HIDDEN
HISTORY
of
NORTH
ALABAMA

HIDDEN HISTORY
of
NORTH ALABAMA

JACQUELYN PROCTER REEVES

Charleston   London

THE
History
PRESS

Published by The History Press
Charleston, SC 29403
www.historypress.net

First published 2010
Second printing 2011

Manufactured in the United States

ISBN 978.1.59629.752.4

Library of Congress Cataloging-in-Publication Data

Reeves, Jacquelyn Procter.
Hidden history of North Alabama / Jacquelyn Procter Reeves.
p. cm.
ISBN 978-1-59629-752-4
1. Alabama--History, Local--Anecdotes. 2. Alabama--Biography--Anecdotes. I. Title.
F326.6.R44 2010
976.1--dc22
2010011265

To three women who made a difference in my life:
Raneé Pruitt, Pat Lewis and Virginia Cook.

Contents

Preface

It is difficult to write a book about history that is unbiased. Readers are left to wonder what is true and what isn't and, most likely, make their own judgments in the end. The best way to make a decision is to be informed of all facts and temper them with common sense. In the end, perhaps it doesn't even matter. Some of us study history for entertainment. But we also realize that what we learn in school is rarely the whole story. Schoolbooks tend to hit the highlights, important facts, and quickly move on. A scratch beneath the surface reveals the story behind the story, and those are the facts we are most likely to remember. Those are the stories I share with you.

There are many people who have helped me tremendously. I can always count on the people at the Archives Department at the Huntsville-Madison County Public Library: Raneé Pruitt, Thomas Hutchens and Susanna Leberman. The service they provide to patrons of the library cannot be measured, and their willingness to share their extensive knowledge with anyone and everyone is much appreciated.

I would also like to thank Patrick Hood for allowing me to use his fabulous photograph of the Forks of Cypress. His other pictures, masterpieces all, are on his website: www.patrickhoodphotographer.com.

I am also forever indebted to Chuck and Jo Shaffer, owners of *Old Tennessee Valley Magazine*, whose generosity is beyond measure. I would also like to thank Robert Gamble, senior architectural historian with the Alabama Historical Commission, for his help and expertise. His knowledge never ceases to amaze me! My thanks to friends Jim and Linda Maples, who support all my endeavors, sound and otherwise, and also to my husband, Robert, who plays devil's advocate in order to make me try harder.

Thanks, too, to the many people at The History Press who have become friends in the process of giving birth to a new book. I'm glad we met!

Finally, I would like to thank the ladies of the Mooresville Brick Church Choir for much-needed comic relief!

SCItanic

O n the morning of Saturday, July 7, 1984, the heat from the Alabama
sun was already oppressive as it made its way up into the sky. The
morning dew turned to a blanket of steam, drawing the very breath from
one's lungs. It seemed to be a perfect day to head to the Tennessee River
for a boat ride, catch a cooling breeze and enjoy the company of friends
and co-workers. That was exactly what second-shift employees of the
South Parkway branch of SCI, an electronics manufacturing company in
Huntsville, planned to do that day.

Employees of the Products Division Plant #2 and their families were
invited for a leisurely excursion on the company boat, a one-hundred-foot
paddle-wheeler given the tongue-in-cheek name *SCItanic* in a contest held
to name the boat—an eerie referral to the passenger ship that had perished
in the icy Atlantic waters earlier in the century. Another SCI department
was originally assigned use of the *SCItanic* on that day but had traded with
members of the Products Division, whose workers had more kids and were
eager to take the ride in the daytime as opposed to the more romantic
evening cruise scheduled for that night. Although eighty-two people were
expected that day, only fifteen showed up, plus a crew of three, including the
captain, Frank May, who had a commercial ship pilot's license. They would
leave from Ditto Landing.

Ditto Landing took the name from a white settler from North Carolina,
John Ditto, who arrived in the early 1800s and operated a ferry across the
Tennessee River, a 652-mile-long tributary of the Ohio River. John Ditto

played an active role in the American Revolution; however, he supported the British. As a result, he left his home state after a number of disputes with his neighbors ended in lawsuits. He came into the territory that would later become Alabama and coexisted peacefully with local Chickasaw Indians as he established his trading post and ferry business.

The Tennessee River, once known as the Cherokee River, dips deeply into northern Alabama, providing fertile soil for the many cotton farmers and recreational opportunities for boaters and fishermen. Hobbs Island skirts the outermost edge of the river near Ditto Landing. The riverbank at Ditto Landing was, and is, a scenic location for picnics, cookouts and camping. The sparkling waters of the river, framed by hardwoods and evergreens against a backdrop of the Appalachian foothills, promised to provide, on July 7, 1984, a pleasant setting for a cruise.

Captain May checked the weather forecast early that morning and confirmed what he thought would be a good day for an outing on the six-year-old boat, originally named *Dixie Darling*. At 5:30 a.m., the forecast predicted a 30 percent chance of thunderstorms with northerly winds at ten miles per hour and a high of ninety degrees. By 9:30 a.m., when the passengers were beginning to assemble at Ditto Landing to board the *SCItanic*, the forecast had changed slightly. The radar indicated a band of storms moving from the southeast into North Alabama.

All was well. Guests eagerly anticipated the trip, and there were smiles all around when the boat was launched at about 10:20 a.m. Soon, clouds began to gather in the sky. Captain May spotted a lightning strike in the distance. It was just after 11:00 a.m., and the captain turned up the volume on the NOAA weather radio in time to hear that there was a severe thunderstorm warning issued for Madison and Morgan Counties. May turned the boat around and announced that they would be returning to Ditto Landing. Suddenly the rains came, carried by seventy-mile-per-hour winds, and began to fall in torrents. The passengers rushed into the cover of the salon as the visibility through the curtain of rain dropped from seven miles down to three miles. Only three minutes had passed since the warning on the weather station.

Crew member Marliana Cressey asked if any of the passengers wanted a life preserver; some said they did and quickly strapped them on. The sky darkened ominously, and within only a few minutes, the visibility dropped again to three-quarters of a mile. Still, the captain and crew remained calm. The boat was made to withstand one-hundred-mile-per-hour winds and had made excursions nearly every day since it was purchased by SCI eighteen months earlier.

The *SCItanic* was now headed into the wind. The sky was black, and the noise from the driving wind was deafening. Captain May had the boat less than one mile away from the marina when he felt something slam into the side. He was knocked violently to the floor but managed to grab the radio microphone and key it. "Mayday!" he shouted, and suddenly he was under water.

The passengers lost their footing as the ship began to topple over. Crew members shouted, "Grab a life jacket! Come to the high side!" in an effort to redistribute the weight and keep the ship afloat. Marliana Cressey didn't have time to shout the orders again. She wondered for a split second if she should jump into the water. The rail of the ship was coming fast over her head as if the whole ship was spinning around her. She struggled to open the salon door, but it was sealed shut by the relentless wind. There was no way to get to the high side. Everyone around her was screaming; one woman reached for her husband as he was pulled away, downward into the rushing water.

A man in a small boat had passed the *SCItanic* just a few minutes before. He, too, was caught by surprise in the thunderstorm. His boat was tossed about like a toy and slammed into the trees lining the shore. As he struggled to gain control, he managed to look over his left shoulder as the *SCItanic* rose up in the water, paused for only a moment and rolled to starboard. In just a second, it was completely capsized.

There was chaos and confusion as the passengers, now trapped in the salon under water, tried to get out. Some people tried to break the windows with chairs, but their struggles were useless. Captain May swam to the surface and reached for survivors as they clawed their way above water. He pulled them onto the bottom of the pontoons, now above the swirling water. One woman struggled as the water filled her lungs. She heard a voice telling her to open her eyes. When she did, she saw light above her, and the voice told her to follow it. The voice had led her to safety. The time was 11:25 a.m., only fifteen minutes after the captain heard the thunderstorm warning on his radio and twelve minutes after the rain first began to fall.

Rescuers rushed to the scene of the accident. Units from the Huntsville police department, the Madison County sheriff's department, the army, the Coast Guard, marine police and various civilians quickly worked together to assess the scene. About fifteen divers dove time and time again into the murky waters with flashlights, struggling to see past the churned-up river soil in search of possible victims. Police had roped off the walkway to the marina to make way for the bodies that were being recovered and to keep away the distraught family members and gawkers.

By 12:30 p.m., five bodies had been recovered, but there were more to come. One woman was told not to give up hope that her husband had survived, but she had seen a stretcher with a body on it, partially covered with a sheet. She recognized her husband's boot. She knew.

The weather continued to hamper recovery efforts. More than one inch of rain fell over the course of a few hours, and marble-sized hail was reported in Toney, Alabama, at 2:15 p.m. Lightning strikes blew out transformers and knocked down power lines, leaving many homes without power for some time. Two storms moved through quickly, followed by two more.

Only four passengers and the three members of the crew survived the accident. Finally, the bodies of the eleven remaining passengers were recovered. All had been trapped in the salon. The leisurely two-hour excursion had turned into the deadliest boating accident in the recorded history of Alabama's inland waterways.

Days later, the crew of a helicopter flying over the area reviewed the extensive damage the weather had caused to the area near Ditto Landing. Trees were gnarled, twisted and snapped; buildings were destroyed, and several around the area had burned to the ground, possibly due to lightning strikes. The storms had left their mark on Huntsville and Madison County, but it was nothing like the tolls taken from the families of the victims of the *SCItanic*. Their lives would never be the same. Four members of one family had died, leaving a fifteen-year-old as the sole survivor because he had been out of the country. Another family lost three members; their enormous grief was shared by the entire city of Huntsville. But along with the grief came the questions of how and why. It wasn't long until people began to point fingers of blame, and within days, the litigators and lawsuits began to line up.

The overturned *SCItanic* was pulled from its watery grave and taken to Florence by a salvage company. An investigation was launched to determine the cause of the accident and assign blame. Tests were made to determine the center of gravity and any other possible causes of the capsizing. The immediate explanation seemed to be the freakish weather. It was not a tornado, as some had suggested, although the winds were measured at seventy-one miles per hour. (Hurricane winds are defined as seventy-four miles per hour and higher.) But soon, another explanation was offered. Until that time, most people had never heard the term "microburst," but now it was used to describe the cause of the accident. A sudden downward gust of air, coming from the southeast, had hit the broadside of the boat and, in essence, shoved it over. According to the findings issued by the Coast Guard study, the microburst phenomenon was first identified in 1978 to describe extreme types of wind shear that involves a narrow, downward and rapidly approaching column of air. Captain May and SCI Systems were cleared of any wrongdoing in the deaths of eleven people.

The lawsuits continued, however, and while one claim was settled out of court rather quickly, it took years to settle the remaining cases. Litigants asked for total amounts of $130 million and claimed that there should have been a capsize plan for the safety of the passengers. One suit claimed that the boat was essentially a top-heavy mobile home on pontoons. On March 19, 1987, nearly three years after the *SCItanic* tragedy, newspapers announced that the last of the lawsuits had finally been settled out of court.

The Rise and Fall of Russel Erskine

O n the morning of March 15, 1938—the Ides of March—eighteen
Army Air Corps pilots, under the command of Captain D.M. Allison,
rumbled out of Selfridge Field in Harrison Township, Michigan. Their
destination was Tampa, Florida. As the day wore on, the Seversky P-35s
of the Seventeenth Pursuit Squadron flew over Huntsville, Alabama, and
took note of the sign on top of Huntsville's only skyscraper, the twelve-story
Hotel Russel Erskine. They headed south with the intention of making a
short refueling stop at Maxwell Air Force Base in Montgomery.

As they continued on their journey, the wind picked up and the sky turned
an ominous black. Rain began to fall in violent torrents and tossed the planes
around like toys. The pilots did not know it then, but on that day, twenty-two
tornadoes would bring death and destruction throughout the region.

As the P-35 fuel gauges warned the pilots that they were perilously close
to empty, the men realized that it would be impossible to safely land in the
stormy weather. They remembered the relatively clear sky over Huntsville
and turned their planes around, not knowing what they would do when they
got there.

It was early evening when they reached Huntsville and flew close overhead,
circling the town in search of a solution. Although Huntsville had a runway
of sorts, there was no control tower and no runway lights. Fortunately for
the pilots, two astute police officers looked up into the sky and realized that
the planes were in trouble. The officers hurried to a local radio station and
issued a plea for all in the listening area to drive down to the airport runway

and park their cars in such a way that their headlights would illuminate the landing strip. The residents of Huntsville responded. Carloads of people quickly drove to the landing strip and waited with excitement, no doubt aware of the potential danger to themselves and their families.

With their headlights shining on the primitive runway, the grateful pilots saw the answer to their prayers unfold before them. As they circled in formation, Captain Allison was the first to peel out and come in for a landing. Everyone on the ground watched intently as the plane swooped down and bumped onto the ground, skidding to a safe stop. Captain Allison then directed the remaining seventeen planes down to the safety and comfort of solid ground. One by one, the others landed as observers held their breaths and cheered with every successful landing. Finally, the last pilot made his descent. Just before the moment of touchdown, a gust of wind caught under one wing and threatened to flip the plane over. In a split second, the pilot made the decision to make another circle and try again. The plane lifted shakily up into the sky and circled once again. This time he was successful and landed his P-35 to whoops, hollers and cheers all around.

One of the relieved pilots was heard to remark that he was hoping not to have to land in one of those grits fields. The pilots, all heroes in the eyes of Huntsville, were escorted to stay the night in Huntsville's finest hotel, the Russel Erskine.

The Hotel Russel Erskine was finished in 1928. It was the finest hotel in all of North Alabama, and the furnishings, food and rooms were top quality. Its namesake, Huntsville native Russel Erskine, came from his home in South Bend, Indiana, for the grand opening. Some sources say that originally the hotel was to be named in honor of Confederate/U.S. general Joseph Wheeler, but the financiers ran out of money before the hotel was completed. Financiers asked Russel Erskine to chip in for the rest of the cost. He did so on the condition that the name be changed to honor him instead of Joe Wheeler. Another version says that the hotel was named for him in the hope that he would contribute money. When he arrived for the grand opening, he was wined and dined, but he left without opening his wallet.

The Rise and Fall of Russel Erskine

Russel Erskine, born in Huntsville in 1871, descended from fine stock. His maternal ancestor, Lieutenant Albert Russel, fought in the American Revolution, and his home stood on what is still known as Russel Hill, though it is frequently misspelled with two *l*'s. His daughter married into the Erskine family, and the name Albert Russel Erskine was used in successive generations.

The subject of our story dropped out of school at age fifteen to sell apples to passengers who came through town on the train. Russel Erskine became a paid employee of the railroad and, by keeping his nose to the grindstone and going through the ranks, went on to become a bank president. He then worked for Studebaker Automobile, first as treasurer and, eventually, as president. He built a fine estate in South Bend, Indiana, and gave a nod to his hometown in Huntsville when his estate was named Twyckenham, a slightly modified version of the first historic district in Huntsville called Twickenham.

Albert Russel Erskine, known to most people as Russel, was making quite a mark on history already. When he went to Studebaker in 1911, the company was in transition from manufacturing wagons to gasoline-powered automobiles (horseless carriages). Erskine started as treasurer of the company, but by 1915, he was president. It was the only company to make the successful transition to motorized vehicles. In 1920, 51,000 automobiles were sold; by 1923, that number had increased to an impressive 150,000. In 1927, the smaller Erskine automobile was introduced—the jaunty forerunner of the compact cars that were becoming popular in Europe—but it was only produced for three years.

Albert Russel Erskine was on top of the world. His motto was "we eat obstacles for breakfast." His personal worth was estimated at $12 to $15 million, and he was awarded with many shares of Studebaker stock. He served as president of the board of lay trustees of Notre Dame University and designated an annual award to the finest college football team called the Albert Russel Erskine Award. In addition, $10,000 was given by Studebaker, every year, to Harvard University to establish the Albert Russel Erskine Bureau for Street Traffic Research.

In 1929, all was well with Studebaker Automobile. It had success with several six-cylinder touring car lines: the Big Six, the Light Six and the Special Six, followed by the classic and regal eight-cylinder President 8. It offered features such as ragtops, mother-in-law (or rumble) seats, wooden spoke wheels and wide whitewall tires. The Studebaker line was a step up from Ford's Model Ts and Model As; it was a favorite of the wealthier class, who were willing to pay more for luxury and innovation.

Studebaker automobile. *Library of Congress.*

But the world came plummeting down in October of that same year with the stock market crash, followed by the Great Depression. Studebaker's working capital went from $36 million in 1926 to $3.5 million in 1932. Automobiles were still considered luxury items in those days, and although Studebaker survived the first few years of the Depression, by 1933, the company had gone into receivership. Russel Erskine, with his wealth and status in serious trouble, his stock worthless and his career yanked from under him, went into the bedroom of his Twyckenham Estate on July 1, 1933, put a towel over his chest and shot himself through the heart. He left two suicide notes, one for his grown son and the other for his attorney, that read, "Nervous system shattered, cannot go on." Conspicuously absent was a note for his wife.

One source claimed that Russel Erskine's insurance policy was due to lapse, and in order to provide for his family financially, he intentionally killed himself in order to get the insurance payoff. The insurance money paid his outstanding debts but left little else to live on.

Russel Erskine's body was brought to Huntsville for burial in the Erskine family mausoleum at Maple Hill Cemetery. His wife and adopted son returned to South Bend to live out their lives. It was common knowledge that Mrs. Erskine was not kind to their adopted son. There were rumors, though never substantiated, that their son, Albert Russel Erskine IV, was *his* natural son but not hers. Even so, one record indicates that the adopted son's natural father was from Norway and his natural mother from Sweden.

While locally the name Albert Russel Erskine is mostly known for those who came before him, in South Bend, Indiana, there are many streets and buildings bearing the name Erskine or Twyckenham. He apparently never forgot his hometown. At some point, he bought extra property bordering Maple Hill Cemetery, built the mausoleum and donated the front gate in memory of his mother, Sue Ragland Erskine. Russel Erskine's wife, Anna, was interred at Maple Hill when she died, and the cremated remains of his son were interred at Maple Hill in 2006.

The magnificent Hotel Russel Erskine fell on hard times as well. The hotel's heyday of the 1940s, '50s and '60s disappeared when the bypass known as Memorial Parkway directed traffic to the outskirts of town and away from the heart of downtown. Businesses and motels followed the path of the parkway, and the Hotel Russel Erskine, with its glorious memories, sparkling cut glass goblets and uniformed bellhops, closed. In recent years, the Hotel Russel Erskine has been restored and is now a senior citizens' home. It is also, perhaps, the home of a ghost or two from Huntsville's bygone days.

Revenge

The Life of Jenny Brooks

L ife has a way of surprising us. We expect happiness and success, yet we can't appreciate success without first experiencing failure; we take for granted a warm bed until we sleep out in the cold, true love until after the despair of heartbreak. Some believe that our lives are predestined. Perhaps that is true when one counts milestones, but how we react to those milestones is completely up to us. We are born with our personalities, along with the ability to overcome and improve our destinies. Some use life's lemons to make lemonade. But some, like the legendary Jenny Brooks, live most of their lives under a bitter blanket of revenge. Although accounts of her life do not always agree some 180 years after her story began, and details tend to differ with every telling, the highlights and lowlights are always the same.

Louisa Elisabeth Jane Bates, born in January 1826 in Kentucky, was fourteen years old when she married Willis Brooks, a man twenty-one years her senior. Despite all of her given names, everyone knew her by one name: Aunt Jenny. Her family was prominent in Jefferson and Walker Counties, and although Jenny had the bluest of eyes, she was half Cherokee. By 1850, Jenny and her husband had moved to Lawrence County with their three children. Six more children were born to them, with eighteen years separating the first and the last. The 1860 census for Lawrence County lists Willis Brooks's occupation as a saddler, although most modern-day accounts recall him as a notorious bootlegger.

The year 1861 brought turmoil to our nation and terror to those who lived in harm's way. Confederate forces, vastly outnumbered, had to find creative means to increase their depleted ranks. Units known as home guards roamed throughout the South. They served to protect civilians in much the same way as today's police force. They also searched for deserters from the Confederate army and for fresh recruits (usually unwilling) to fight the Yankees. They were sanctioned by the local government, yet they had no real supervision and frequently abused their powers. They were rarely paid, made their own rules with no recourse and could execute people accused of desertion or aiding the enemy. Some were cruel, others were useless and there were always those who seemed to prey on innocent people as ruthlessly as guerrilla raiders.

The Brooks family lived in the mountains of Lawrence County, now known as Bankhead Forest, and wished for nothing more than to be left alone. They did not own slaves, and they did not wish to fight, but one day in 1864, the War Between the States came to them.

The mountains of North Alabama were reputed to be a safe haven for Confederate deserters sick of the rivers of blood, the stench of death and the gnawing pain in their empty stomachs. According to some sources, a home guard unit made up of eight men arrived at the Brooks home to force the eldest son, John, to enlist. Others sources say that fifty-eight-year-old Willis Brooks was allegedly giving aid to the Union army. Willis was no match for the eight-man posse. He was tortured, strung up by his neck on a tree limb and shot to death. His oldest son, nineteen-year-old John, was shot to death as well. Jenny Brooks, who supposedly witnessed both killings, was overcome with grief but, like many Southern women, found the resolve not only to take control of the situation but also to exact revenge. Jenny Brooks had all of her children place their hands on the dead body of their father and vow not to give up until all eight men were cold in their graves.

Not long after the murders, Jenny and one of her sons shot dead the leader of the home guard, Dr. Andrew Kaiser, at his home. His wife was forced to reveal the names of the other men: Jeff Hogan, Bob South, Mack Gosey, Jim Smith, Hue Lagion, Bill Weams and Sherm Williams. Jenny cut Andrew Kaiser's head off and boiled it in her yard until the flesh was gone. After removing the lower jaw, she used the skull as a washbasin.

Jenny had a hickory stick to keep count of the dead men. She cut notches into the side every time the Brookses brought another one down. Seven notches were eventually cut into the stick, and Jenny claimed to have killed three of the men herself. Some say that the last of the eight men disappeared.

At some point, Jenny married Jacob Stauder Johnston, a widower who moved his children with him into Jenny's home. She was a midwife in the area and used her knowledge of Cherokee medicine to help the sick in the community. If she took a dislike to someone, she became a force to be reckoned with. Anyone running for political office had to receive her personal endorsement to get elected. According to lore, she once went into a store and pulled out a wad of money to pay for her merchandise. The merchant commented on the amount of cash she carried, and she snapped back, "I pay myself twenty dollars a month to mind my own business!"

In the meantime, the Brooks boys gained reputations for their lawlessness. The daughters married men who rode with the Brooks boys. At times, they went to hide out in Texas or Oklahoma with relatives until it was safe to come home. But the lifestyle they chose was about to catch up to them. One by one, the boys died violently. Son Gainam hid in the bushes and shot a deputy to death as he spoke to the Brookses' neighbors, a black family named Hubbard. Henry Hubbard fired his rifle toward the direction of the gunfire and hit his mark. Gainam Brooks stumbled out into the open and died. When Jenny Brooks arrived moments later to find her son's bloody body, she threatened to kill them all—and they knew she meant it. The Hubbard family packed up and left.

In 1884, the *Moulton Advertiser* published a story that accused the Brooks family of, among other things, "general cussedness." According to a Brooks family member, Henry Brooks was sent to Fort Leavenworth for stealing a horse. One of his relatives tried to break him out by bringing him a file hidden in a bucket of syrup. He was caught and sentenced to a year in prison. In the meantime, charges against Henry were dropped, and he was out of prison before his well-meaning relative.

Aunt Jenny outlived all of her sons—her last living son was killed in a moonshine raid—but at the end of her life, she found religion and donated land for a church. Aunt Jenny Brooks Johnston died on March 29, 1924, at the age of ninety-eight and was buried at Poplar Springs Cemetery. According to legend, as she lay on her deathbed, the last thing she wanted was to wash her hands. The skull of the man who had murdered her husband and son was brought to her. Perhaps this macabre gesture signified that she had accomplished her life's goal.

Other versions of the deaths of Willis and John Brooks deserve to be told. Some sources say that they were killed by Yankees, and one story claims that they were killed as a result of an ongoing feud with another family. Moonshine was prevalent in the hills of North Alabama and may have had some role in the murders. We may never know the true facts.

Aunt Jenny Brooks Johnston's name, as well as the stories told about her, are still known far and wide in North Alabama. Unfortunately, her headstone has disappeared, and her home was burned by vandals in October 2005.

The Brooks boys lived and died violently. Perhaps it was their destiny.

The Pride of Courtland

The pride of the assembled crowd was undeniable. Half of the male population of Courtland, Alabama, bearing the hope of the future, was dressed in snappy new uniforms made by the loving hands of the wives, mothers, sisters and sweethearts of their hometown. They called themselves the Red Rovers, and with much excitement and fanfare, they were about to embark on a true adventure of the American spirit. They would save the day, uphold Democracy and preserve every American's God-given rights. But most of them would never see Courtland, Alabama, again.

In the late fall of 1835, Dr. Jack Shackelford, a Virginian by birth and Alabamian by choice, read a plea from General Sam Houston, former governor of Tennessee and now a resident of the Republic of Texas. Houston, commander of the Texas army, asked for volunteers to bring a good rifle and one hundred rounds of ammunition and help their fellow Americans in Texas's fight for independence from Mexico. If they would only come to the aid of their countrymen, they would be rewarded with bounties of land. Who could resist? After all, just over five decades earlier their forefathers had received the same promise to fight the British, and it seemed the genetic disposition toward wanderlust was in every American's heart.

Life on the edge was nothing new to Dr. Shackelford. After moving to Shelby County in 1818 to claim the cure for Alabama Fever, he established a successful medical practice and a comfortable plantation. He ran successfully for political office and was overwhelmingly admired. He lost it all, however, when he guaranteed a loan for a cousin whose business failed. After paying his cousin's debts, and with little of his money left, Shackelford brought his family north to Courtland to start over. The earliest residents of Courtland and the surrounding area were wealthy planters from the upper South who built fine homes and a solid community. Tall red cedars added to the natural beauty of the fertile Tennessee River Valley, and the red soil was conducive to growing quality cotton crops.

Dr. Shackelford did well in Courtland, but perhaps at the age of forty-five he was ready for a new challenge. He was a natural leader, a veteran of the War of 1812 (with a saber scar across his face as a souvenir), and answered the call of duty to help the many men and women out West—most of whom were former residents of Alabama, Tennessee and Kentucky—establish their utopia of choice. Perhaps he saw his own future in Texas.

Shackelford called for a meeting of the townspeople to talk about the plight of the Texans. No doubt he already had a plan in mind, but after hearing convincing pleas from prominent people, one by one, the founding fathers placed hundred-dollar bills on the podium, challenging others to do the same. Eleven one-hundred-dollar bills were supplemented by lesser amounts donated by the citizens to help fund a local militia to fight in Texas. Fifty-five men, including Shackelford's son and two nephews, signed up to follow him to Texas.

Matching shirts of red, green and brown checks were made for the men, and their pants were dyed red. They each had a coonskin cap. Dress uniforms were also made with red velvet caps and coats, white pants and a blue sash. They took the name Red Rovers. On December 12, 1835, the proud residents of Courtland met the men as they climbed aboard the railroad cars of the Tuscumbia, Courtland and Decatur Railroad. They also had a regimental flag that they carried proudly. It was solid blood red. Each had his own hunting knife and a musket from the state arsenal. Upon reaching Tuscumbia by train, they boarded a boat to Paducah, Kentucky, and then went down the Mississippi River to New Orleans. A transfer took them across the Gulf of Mexico, and more than a month after telling their families goodbye, they finally landed, on January 19, 1836, at Matagorda Bay.

Nearby Huntsville provided about seventy members of the Huntsville Volunteers, and they were joined by members of the Mobile Greys, as well as the Alabama Greys from Montgomery. Before long, they joined the ranks of the Red Rovers.

In February 1836, the Red Rovers were sworn in and made their way to Fort Defiance, where they joined the command of Colonel James

Fannin. Including other Alabamians, Fannin's command totaled about four hundred. For the next several weeks, Fannin had his men work to fortify the defenses of Fort Defiance, leaving no time for much-needed training. It had been the plan of military leaders to set up smaller forts along the Mexican army's route as it made its way north into Texas. Unfortunately, the much smaller American forces had little chance of survival against the Mexican army, which outnumbered them many times over. In addition, Colonel Fannin did not enjoy the respect of his subordinates, who recognized his faults in military leadership, as well as the disorganization of the American government in Texas.

On March 9, 1836, Captain Jack Shackelford wrote a letter to his wife. He was not yet aware that the massacre at the Alamo had already taken place. He wrote to his wife that the two hundred or so Texan Americans at the Alamo were outnumbered by a force of about five thousand Mexicans led by General Santa Anna. The Americans had fought them off several times, but without reinforcements, they would not last long. David Crockett, Jim Bowie and others who went into infamy had died several days before. General Santa Anna and his men, high on success, were going after Colonel James Fannin and his men next.

Fannin sent some of his men to help evacuate civilians out of the way of the advancing Mexican army as it marched toward Goliad. When the men did not return, Fannin sent another contingent of men. The first group was already dead; the second group was cut off and unable to return.

In the meantime, Sam Houston ordered Fannin and his men to retreat to Victoria to safety. Fannin delayed the retreat, hoping that the second group of Americans would return. While his men waited, they were harassed by Mexican scouts. Though they repulsed the Mexicans, Fannin and his men were soon confronted by a considerably larger army, which they also managed to force out. Fannin finally issued the order to retreat. Early on March 19, they left the fort, setting fire to it to keep the Mexicans from getting their supplies. After crossing difficult terrain and the San Antonio River, with their horses and oxen utterly exhausted, Fannin ordered them to stop in a vulnerable position to rest. Shackelford argued that their only hope was to continue on to the safety of the trees in spite of their fatigue, but Fannin refused to budge. He also informed Shackelford that reinforcements from Victoria were expected at any moment.

The Mexican army, 2,000 strong, attacked the 275 or so men left in Fannin's command in what would become known as the Battle of Coleto Creek. The mass confusion that followed was the result of many mistakes. Lack of proper training, coupled with their defenseless position, was compounded by overheated cannons, which could not be cooled due to a lack of water. Their lack of numbers completed the chaos. By the end of the day, many of the Americans were dead, dying or wounded. Those who remained refused to leave their wounded brethren because they knew the Mexicans would torture them mercilessly, and so they vowed to stay with them to the end.

The night was long and cold. Fannin's men were thirsty and hungry, and then the rain began to fall. The following day, the Mexicans were ready to fight again. The reinforcements Fannin expected never arrived, but five hundred more men had been added to the ranks of Santa Anna's army. Instead of attacking, however, the Mexicans sent word that they were willing to negotiate. Fannin prepared to meet with Santa Anna. Shackelford told him that if he was to consider surrender, it had to be honorable. If that was not to be, he told Fannin to "come back—our graves are already dug—let us all be buried together."

Colonel Fannin brokered a deal for their surrender that stated that his men would be allowed to leave the Republic of Texas if they gave up peaceably. It seemed too good to be true. They were marched back to Goliad and kept as prisoners in a small burned-out church while Fannin and other officers made arrangements for the men to leave Texas.

One week after the surrender, on March 27—Palm Sunday—Shackelford's men were ordered to pack up their belongings and prepare to leave. They were told they would go to Copano and board ships that would get them closer to their homes, wherever they may be. But Shackelford and another medical doctor, Dr. Joseph H. Barnard, were detained. They became alarmed when they heard gunfire and the screams of their men as they stepped outside the fort. It was an all-out massacre. Some tried to run; others stood tall and faced their executioners. Those who escaped the gunfire were run down by the cavalry, and the wounded were bayoneted or shot as they lay on the ground. In the end, about twenty-seven men escaped, including eight Red Rovers. Among the men who lay dead on the ground were Dr. Shackelford's son and two nephews. Santa Anna had agreed to their conditions of surrender, but he never intended to keep his word.

Colonel Fannin's execution was saved for last. He handed over his watch and money to be sent to his family and asked that his execution be according to his status as the commanding officer. They even agreed to give him a Christian burial. Fannin tied a handkerchief over his own eyes, unbuttoned his own shirt to better reveal his heart and asked that he be shot from a distance far enough away to prevent powder burns from tattooing his skin.

The executioner agreed to meet his request and then put his pistol to Fannin's head and shot him—point blank.

The bodies of the massacred men, including that of Colonel Fannin, were stripped, thrown into piles and set on fire. More than 370 men were killed at Goliad. Dr. Shackelford and Dr. Barnard were spared only because their medical expertise was needed to care for the wounded Mexicans.

Dr. Shackelford was horrified. He begged to be executed as well, rather than face his many friends back home whose sons were now dead. And then there was his wife. He was forced, along with Dr. Barnard, to care for the wounded Mexicans. The partially charred bodies of Fannin and his murdered men were left exposed to the elements and wild animals. They were not buried until two months later.

Dr. Shackelford and Dr. Barnard were eventually taken to San Antonio to nurse the Mexicans wounded at the Alamo. By the time they arrived on April 20, nearly seven weeks after the Alamo, many of the wounded men were already dead. But on the following day, 800 Americans, now livid over the massacres at the Alamo and Goliad, bombarded 1,250 of Santa Anna's men at San Jacinto. Their battle cries said it all: "Remember Goliad! Remember the Alamo!" Their anger was rewarded on that day. About 600 Mexicans were killed, and the rest were taken prisoner. The Americans killed in that battle numbered 9.

Local newspapers carried the news of Santa Anna's capture before that of the massacre at Goliad. Although the capture of Fannin's men was reported, there was still hope that they were alive and would return after Santa Anna's downfall.

In the meantime, Dr. Barnard and Dr. Shackelford escaped from San Antonio. Within four days, they found a Texas regiment and made arrangements to return to their homes. Shackelford wrote to his wife on June 22 from New Orleans and broke the news to her. He didn't know that news of the Goliad Massacre had finally reached Courtland, and a public memorial service had already been held for the Red Rovers, all of whom were presumed dead. When Dr. Shackelford reached Courtland on July 9, he was met by the family and friends of the Rovers, who were hoping that perhaps others had survived. They were surprised to see how Dr. Shackelford had changed. His black hair was now thin and white. He looked far older than his years, and he was painfully skinny. No doubt his heart was broken, for he cried as he told the same crowd that had bid him fond farewell a few months earlier of the deaths of their loved ones. They cried as well.

General Antonio Lopez de Santa Anna, the self-proclaimed dictator of Mexico, had ordered the Goliad Massacre, insisting that one of his officers witness the actual executions. He was captured at San Jacinto, but for some ridiculous and unknown reason, he was released a year later. Santa Anna went on to fight against the Americans during the Mexican War of 1846–48.

Dr. Shackelford later returned to Texas to help family members of the Red Rovers claim military wages and land grants for their service. He died in 1857. The following year, Shackelford County, Texas, was named in his honor.

In March 1857, at the request of the Texas commissioner for deeds, a Huntsville newspaper published the names of the Red Rovers, asking that their heirs make arrangements to claim their land bounties in Texas.

The mass grave containing the bodies of the victims of the Goliad Massacre was unmarked and nearly lost. When Goliad Boy Scouts found charred bones in 1930, experts examined the remains and determined that they were the men killed in 1836. In 1938, a permanent monument was finally erected as a memorial to the Courtland Red Rovers and other victims of the Goliad Massacre.

The Strange Life of the Sleeping Preacher

Constantine Sanders was born in Madison County in 1831. At the age of twenty-three, he became gravely ill while at the home of Mr. and Mrs. Allen Harlow in Elkton, Tennessee, and lingered near death for days. As Mrs. Harlow worked to nurse him back to health, she witnessed the seams in his skull separate, stretching his scalp across the schism. His skull split front to back and side to side, wide enough for her to place her finger inside the schism. Sanders survived, but the effects were long lasting and historic. His condition is perhaps the only case of its kind, and there is no word to describe it. Constantine Sanders, known as the "Sleeping Preacher," suffered for over two decades from a malady that some described as a gift from God while others pronounced it a curse of the devil.

Sanders became a minister of the Cumberland Presbyterian faith. He converted to Christianity in a small thirty- by forty-foot simple frame church located about fourteen miles northwest of Huntsville. The building, once known as the Union Chapel Cumberland Presbyterian Church, was moved to the campus of the University of Alabama in Huntsville in December 1973 and now serves as the student art gallery.

Reverend Constantine Sanders ministered to church members in the Alabama towns of Maysville, Meridianville and Mooresville. At times, he appeared to be in a trance or dozing while sitting bolt upright. Sometimes these events were preceded by debilitating headaches, uncontrollable tremors, blood trickling from his eyes and muscle spasms. His breathing slowed, and on more than one occasion, he was pronounced dead, only to

Reverend Constantine Sanders, the Sleeping Preacher. *Photo courtesy Huntsville–Madison County Public Library.*

begin breathing again. The pressures on his chest were excruciating, and at times he bandaged his eyes because of the pain he suffered from the daylight. Yet he was able to maneuver about the room as if his eyes were open and read from books while his eyes were covered. He spoke of occurrences far away—a death, a fire, the location of a lost article or the contents of a sealed letter. Even though Reverend Sanders had a very limited education, while in these trances, he wrote and spoke in languages he had never studied. These events, and many more, were witnessed by a number of reliable people.

As word spread about the inexplicable powers of Reverend Sanders, he began to feel the need to separate fact from fiction and put an end to the many rumors. He sanctioned his friend, Reverend G.W. Mitchell of Athens, to write a book about him. In 1876, it was published with the approval and help of Reverend Sanders.

This book explained the phenomenon in great detail. A secondary personality, which referred to itself as X+Y=Z, served as the voice that manifested itself during Reverend Sanders's trances. It was a personality that did not seem to appreciate Reverend Sanders and referred to Sanders as "my casket." X+Y=Z gave no explanation for the name, the reason for its presence or why Reverend Sanders was so afflicted. The original book contained many accounts of reliable eyewitnesses. For reasons unknown today, Reverend Sanders wanted the books recalled after a second printing in 1877. The unsold books were gathered together in Mooresville and burned. Fortunately, a few copies survived.

In 1981, the original book was reprinted, along with much more information gleaned by Big Cove resident William P. Drake. The late Mr. Drake wrote the final chapters of Reverend Sanders's life and included much interesting information about the people mentioned in the original book.

Reverend Sanders had no warning or control over what happened to him. While riding on the train one day, he fell into a trance. He had no pencil or paper with him, and so he commenced to write on the palm of his hand with the index finger of his other hand. When he had finished, he walked over to another passenger and asked who had sent the letter she was reading. She did not want to answer the question, but Reverend Sanders said that X+Y=Z had written a copy of the letter while she was reading it. He quoted excerpts from the letter, seemingly unaware that it was "written" on the palm of his hand with no pencil.

On one occasion, Reverend Sanders was in a carriage with several people. Soon after falling into his trance, he asked the carriage driver to stop. He stepped out onto the ground, walked a few feet into the woods and was approached by a wild fox. To everyone's surprise, he crouched down and began to pet the fox as if it were a pet.

His friends soon grew accustomed to the strange happenings. Some were amused and enjoyed testing his abilities. Once, while in Tullahoma, Tennessee, Reverend Sanders had returned to the home of friends after they had all attended a church service that went late into the night. Reverend Sanders was in what was described as his nervous sleep as a passenger train passed through the town. Sanders was beginning to describe a heart ailment suffered by one of the train's passengers when he excitedly said that a man wearing a cap was standing on the passenger platform and had accidentally dropped a silver coin onto the ground. When someone asked where the man was from, Reverend Sanders said, "From a paper in his pocket, he is from New York." Sanders then said that the coin had an advertisement on one side and led them to the spot where the coin was found.

On the late evening of April 3, 1876, Reverend Sanders summoned people to the house, and while in his trance, he looked past them and instructed them to go to a certain place in the road; there they would find a two-and-a-half-dollar gold piece. He went with them for a short way and then stopped. The moonlight did not provide enough light for their search, and candles were brought. Reverend Sanders returned to the house while others continued the search. They returned sometime later, empty-handed. Reverend Sanders had been talking to the women who stayed behind, and at one point, he laughed as he described one man crawling around on his hands and knees. Sanders told this same man that while he was searching, he had actually stepped on the coin three times. With the edge of his boot, he had knocked the coin loose, and it was left standing on edge, at a forty-five-degree angle. In addition, Sanders said that a government emblem was on the exposed side. The other side, he said, was partially defaced. The next morning, the men returned, and to their surprise, the coin was exactly as Reverend Sanders described it. Boot prints around it seemed to support his story. An American eagle was on the most visible side. The defaced side was due to someone soldering a fastener onto the back to turn it into a piece of jewelry.

In the spring of 1874, Reverend Sanders visited a friend in Huntsville. He looked forward to hearing Reverend F.A. Ross deliver a sermon at the Cumberland Presbyterian Church that evening. Some hours before the service was to begin, Sanders began to experience the beginnings of another trance. With regret, he left the home of H.R. Smith immediately to return to his home, some twelve miles away. Early the next morning, Reverend Sanders arrived in Huntsville on the train and went back to the home of his friend, Mr. Smith. Sanders gave Smith the outline of Reverend Ross's sermon, including a great many details. He had not been *physically* present at the church service, nor had he talked to anyone else who was there. At the very moment Reverend Ross stood at the pulpit, Reverend Sanders was at home, busily writing the text of the sermon on a sheet of paper. His wife witnessed these events, and Reverend Ross confirmed the contents of his sermon.

Reverend Sanders and the entity that shared his body had two distinct personalities. At times, X+Y=Z needed to communicate to Reverend Sanders and addressed writings to him, calling him "my casket." They were always signed "X+Y=Z." The time came when Reverend Sanders received a letter, written by his own hand, from the entity. It was a letter announcing that he would soon be free of X+Y=Z, along with advice and a promise that X+Y=Z would return. The letter read, in part:

Seventeenth day, 2nd month, 19th century
A.M. 5876, A.D. 1876, 1. P.M.

To my Casket, this message comes greeting. Having so often of late witnessed your groaning with such earnestness to be freed from what seems to you a burden, not that you would be unclothed but clothed upon, these words I now write unto thee in the Lord Jesus.

I charge thee, therefore, before God and the Lord Jesus Christ, who shall judge the quick and the dead at his appearing and his kingdom, Preach the word; be instant in season, out of season; reprove, rebuke, exhort with all long-suffering and doctrine. For the time will come when they will not endure sound doctrine; but after their own lusts shall they heap to themselves teachers, having itching ears, and they turn away their ears from the truth, and shall be turned unto fables. But watch thou in all things, endure afflictions, do the work of an evangelist, make full proof of thy ministry. For I am now ready to be offered and the time of my departure is at hand… Till I come, give attendance to reading, to exhortation, to doctrine. Neglect not the gift that is in thee, which was given thee by prophecy, with the laying on of the hands of the presbytery.

On May 5, 1876, at 4:00 a.m., another letter was written by X+Y=Z, directed to Reverend Sanders:

After twenty-two years of labor and suffering in and through the person of my Casket, and for many years of that time both a mystery and reproach to others, I now come to the end of my first engagement; and will here leave off, in part, the work until my second and last coming, at which time I will reappear to finish up the great work for which I was intended…My Casket, I now come to address you, personally, before I depart. You have been to me greatly a submissive servant, in suffering, in contempt, in wonder, in reproach, by night and by day, from year to year past. You can never fully see all you have passed in this life until you see the life to come, when then you stand ready to fall back to dust, whence you came; and I leave you forever. I have given you many valuable lessons, and prevented you from many difficulties and sorrows. I have shown you many friends, and many foes; what their strength and how to treat them. Together we have dwelt in peace and safety; but at your request, I leave you for a time. Till I come your head will remain the seat of great pain; and at times to you almost unbearable. But be humble, and also patient. And amid the sympathy of friends, may God help you to be submissive.

Your entire body will be, of necessity, the dwelling place of powerful electric force; but this will help to keep you up, and make you useful in many ways to others.

My books and papers, I leave in your charge; but these you are, on no account, to exhibit till I come. In this be faithful. Give earnest heed.

Examine the sick of body, and by reference to my books, give relief when you can.

Examine the sick of soul, and, by aid of the truth, give relief to them if possible.

You will often and sadly miss me, when I am gone, but you cannot realize it now.

My former "charge" I leave with you; and would say; Fill up the measure thereof that I may return to you the sooner.

With Heaven's benediction I will now bid you adieu.

William Pickens Drake, the author of the 1981 edition, added a letter that was not available at the first printing. This letter helped answer questions about the affliction of Reverend Sanders, yet it opened the door for many more that may never be answered. It was also written by the X+Y=Z entity:

My peculiar developments will not be explained from a scientific stand-point, at least so long as it is assumed that my physical sufferings are the cause of my mental phenomena. The solution may be sought successfully, only from a theological and scriptural stand-point. I am no spiritist nor clairvoyant; neither am I the subject of mesmerism or animal-magnetism. But I am a "vessel of mercy" whom the Lord hath chosen to this end. And I will in after days explain the difference between these terms and the office I fill.

In the fall of 1876, the original volume was closed out with the words of the first author, G.W. Mitchell. It explained that many of the predictions had come to pass, and that, as of that time, there had been no reappearance of the X+Y=Z entity. As of now, there doesn't seem to be a record of the return of X+Y=Z, nor has there ever been a plausible explanation for the strange occurrences in the life of Reverend Constantine Sanders.

Reverend Sanders died on Good Friday, April 14, 1911, and was buried at the edge of Stevenson City Cemetery on Easter Sunday. He was seventy-nine years old. His lengthy obituary described many aspects of his life and his faith, but conspicuous in its absence is any reference to the X+Y=Z entity that occupied his body and mind for some twenty-two years. The obituary went on to say that he preached over ten thousand sermons and was survived by his wife of over fifty years, two sons and two daughters. His wife, Duenna White Sanders, died two and a half years later. Their simple headstones, devoid of answers to the many questions that remain about their lives, bear only dates and names.

Stars Fell on Alabama

From the years 2002 to 2009, the words "Stars Fell on Alabama" were emblazoned across the license plates of Alabama drivers. Few people, however, are aware of the fascinating story behind the slogan.

Mild temperatures were appreciated and enjoyed by residents of Alabama in the fall of 1833. Cotton was in from the fields, and the respite from the brutal summer heat would lead, within a few short weeks, to the chilly winter winds. The subdued sunlight had already signaled the leaves to drop from the trees, leaving jagged, yet graceful limbs climbing upward for warmth. Earlier in the year, President Andrew Jackson had begun his second term in office. The news all over the United States and Europe buzzed about the abolition of slavery in the British Empire.

On the evening of November 12, 1833, all over North Alabama residents went to sleep as they did every night. The sky was particularly clear. But sometime after midnight, one by one, people began to take note of something happening outside, high in the sky. Shooting stars streaked across the inky black sky. It was beautiful, even romantic—at first. But the few stars that fell every minute came faster, larger and stronger. Hundreds upon hundreds began to fill the evening sky.

Those who had already gone to sleep were soon awakened, if not from the gradual light filling their windows, then from the cries of their neighbors, who were overcome with ever-increasing fear. Men at gaming houses, the illegal gambling establishments that conducted business late into the night, began to worry that it was a sign from the heavens signaling the destruction of the world. In the time that remained—perhaps only a few moments, they feared—they felt the desperate need to atone for their sins. Men confessed their indiscretions, admitted to crimes they planned to commit and professed their immediate salvation. The warming fires in fireplaces were filled with playing cards hastily tossed into the flames. Some hid under tables as if they could hide from the Judgment.

In Lauderdale County, Alabama, slaves who lived at Woodland Plantation (some accounts report that it was Woodlawn, though no evidence of a plantation of that name could be found) were also filled with fear. Outside of their cabins, they rolled on the ground, cried and prayed to Almighty God and the heavens above. It was the end of time, it was the end of slavery and yet it was death. The mistress of the plantation rushed out into the darkness to see what could be done. She read from the Bible in an attempt to calm them, but their anxieties increased as the streaks of light kept coming. Was it one of the warnings from the Book of Revelation that the end of time was near?

Nothing the woman said had any impact, except to make the situation worse. In short order, her husband, the master of the plantation, stomped out of the home, and he was boiling mad! He cursed and bellowed with every breath. The slaves turned their eyes to him, perhaps expecting him to be struck dead by a lightning bolt. Strangely enough, his profanity calmed their fears. After all, if the master wasn't worried that taking the Lord's name in vain would condemn him to eternal flames, then perhaps it wasn't the end of time after all. And they were right. By morning, everyone assumed that the activity of the meteor storm had subsided. In reality, the meteorites continued but were obscured by daylight.

It was later decided that the storm was particularly brilliant in the eastern portion of the United States. The stars seemed to emanate from the constellation Leo, seen high in the eastern sky. In fact, Leo served simply as the vanishing point—the storm did not come from Leo at all—yet it will always be known as the Leonid Meteor Shower. Men of wisdom blamed the shooting stars on weather, yet while some explained that it was caused by dry air, others said it was damp air. It was too cold, it was too warm, it was everything—and yet it was nothing.

The phenomenon was discussed at length for weeks. Everyone shared their fears, where they were and what was said. In fact, it was discussed so much that for many years, time was marked by this celestial event, and remembrances of times past would be described as having happened either before the stars fell or after.

Woodland Plantation in Lauderdale County. *HABS-HAER photograph.*

It would take years for scientists and astronomers to complete their studies and report their findings, but the meteor storm known as the Leonid Meteor Shower was not a one-time event. The brilliant shower seen that night happens every 33.25 years, the time it takes for the earth to intersect with the elliptical orbit of the tail of a comet that carries debris, ice, rocks and even pebbles and sand. Like Earth, these meteorites orbit the sun, but the elliptical shape of the orbit ensures that, eventually, Earth will enter the orbit. When this happens, at the very least, we have another brilliant meteor storm. Yet we can still see, to a lesser extent, shooting stars from the meteor shower every November. But there was no visible sign of the Leonids in 1899 or 1933; scientists admit that there is still much to learn.

For most people, the facts regarding the vastness of space and all of its mysteries are difficult to grasp. The shooting stars seen in the 1833 Leonid Meteor Shower were actually the lights from comet dust dating back to 1800. It took thirty-three years for the light to reflect back to Earth.

The meteor storm may have been forgotten altogether had it not been for a writer by the name of Carl Carmer who wrote of his years spent in Alabama in a book called *Stars Fell on Alabama*. It was published in 1934, the same year Frank Perkins and Mitchell Parish wrote a song by the same title. The song, with its sweet melody and romantic words, is still played and sung by many Alabama college choir students, ensuring that the stars will continue to fall on Alabama for decades to come.

A Military Occupation of a Different Kind

At 9:40 p.m. on February 15, 1898, a fiery explosion filled the darkened sky in Havana Harbor. The USS *Maine*, a 6,682-ton, second-class battleship filled with more than five tons of gunpowder, blew sky-high. Through roiling clouds of flames and black smoke fell debris of metal, burning wood and bloody body parts of more than 260 men whose torn remains sank into watery graves. After a short and less than thorough investigation, the explosion of the ship was blamed on Spanish terrorists who had been sent to Cuba to quell an insurrection. Stories of Spain's torture and oppression of Cuban citizens had decent Americans screaming for justice. While the American government was hesitant to get involved in an international dispute, the USS *Maine* had been sent to warn the Spanish government that American citizens living in Cuba had better be left alone. Cuba was struggling for independence from Spain, and the seditious details reported by the media set the stage for the events to come.

Although several plausible explanations for the explosion were suggested, American outrage began to snowball, growing faster and larger as it rolled into the nation's capital. Was it sabotage? Was it an explosive mine? It didn't seem to matter, the result was the same. The one thing eyewitnesses agreed on was that there were two distinct explosions, seconds apart. "Remember the *Maine*— to hell with Spain!" became a rallying cry. And so, on April 25, two months after the explosion, the United States declared war on Spain.

Assistant Secretary of the Navy Theodore Roosevelt worried that there would be few men to volunteer to fight, but he was wrong. The War Department was inundated with volunteers, and Roosevelt resigned from his position to serve as second in command under his friend Leonard Wood, of the famed cavalry unit that would become known as the Rough Riders.

Military leaders used some practical insight to determine battle strategy. Knowing that the tropical climate of Cuba would be a detriment to U.S. soldiers, much recruiting was done in the southwestern states where residents were more accustomed to higher temperatures. As a result, the Rough Riders were a curious mixture of ranch hands, gold prospectors, lawmen, Indians, bandits, former Civil War soldiers and even some Ivy League college boys from the East who were right at home on polo ponies. The challenge, so it seemed, was to get the diverse soldiers to bond. By the end of May, hastily trained recruits made their way to Tampa, Florida, where they would board ships and head to Cuba.

The sentiments across the United States had certainly changed from a few decades earlier. As the men traveled from their homes to Florida, preparing to set sail for the conflict ahead of them, many noticed that old wounds inflicted some thirty-five years earlier in the War Between the States were beginning to heal. City boys from Boston rode alongside country boys from Tennessee, wearing the same uniform and cheered on by the same people, who waved the same flag. Confederate veterans, stooped over with age and infirmity, smiled wistfully at these young men as they passed by and shouted words of encouragement. There was, for the first time in decades, a sense of unity. And with that unity came a renewed sense of American pride.

But although more than three decades had passed, the fears of the mothers and wives were the same. Their expressions were identical in every war, every conflict. They could not hide the worry in their eyes, the sadness and dread that came with knowing that wars were not fought without great sacrifice of human life. The blood of their loved ones would soak the soil of a strange land, and God forbid, perhaps their bones would lie in unmarked graves forevermore. It was all too much.

Alabama was represented well by a Georgia transplant by the name of Joe Wheeler. Even though he was sixty-two years old, and despite the fact that, as a former Confederate general, he (officially) once bore arms against the U.S. government, he was determined to participate. Wheeler had been a Rebel to the bone and had even been imprisoned after the Civil War. He earned the nickname "Fightin' Joe" while stationed in the New Mexico Territory before the Civil War. While he was escorting a caravan of civilians along the Santa Fe Trail, Indians attacked the covered wagons. Joe fought with all his might, firing his Colt pistols until the Indians abandoned their plans.

After the Civil War years, Wheeler settled down to married life at his Pond Springs, Alabama home and entered politics. He could have spent his golden

A Military Occupation of a Different Kind

General Joseph Wheeler as a young man. *Photo courtesy Huntsville–Madison County Public Library.*

years retelling war stories and planning his next political campaign, but the call of battle appealed to his deep sense of service. Washington politicians relented, and General Joe Wheeler took command once again.

THE BUFFALO SOLDIERS

When the War Between the States broke out, approximately 180,000 slaves enlisted to fight for the Union army. There are estimates that about 33,000 of the total 620,000 men who died in the war had been slaves.

In 1866, Congress passed a law to form two all-black cavalry and four all-black infantry regiments. Many of the all-black regiments, nicknamed the Buffalo Soldiers, were stationed in the Midwest and Southwest, where they came into contact with Indians, and it was the Cheyennes and Comanches who gave them the name. It was, on one hand, a sign of respect because the Indians admired the wooly buffalo that roamed the open country; on the other hand, the Indians thought the black soldiers' hair resembled the coat of the shaggy beast. Some say they were given the name because they wore buffalo hides to keep warm during the bitter winter months. A large number of the Buffalo Soldiers had been slaves on Texas cattle ranches before the Civil War, and many others had either been born into slavery or were sons of former slaves.

While stationed in the Southwest, the Buffalo Soldiers worked to map the dust-blown Great Plains with their fields of lava rock and petrified sharks' teeth from prehistoric times. The Buffalo Soldiers also put up telegraph wires, helped build frontier outposts and protected the railroad men from hostile Indians led by the likes of Geronimo, Sitting Bull, Chief Victorio and Lone Wolf. The men who laid the tracks for the iron horse to chug out west also had to contend with thieves and outlaws.

In Lincoln County, New Mexico, trouble was brewing. Two factions formed in support of the two merchants in the tiny town of Lincoln. There were ranchers and their hired hands on one side against ranchers and their hired hands on the other side. In the fall of 1877, Englishman John Tunstall was murdered. Over the next few months, there were retaliatory murders, and in the summer of 1888, a full-blown range war erupted with the infamous Billy the Kid in the middle of the fray.

The Buffalo soldiers, who were stationed at Fort Stanton, were sent to Lincoln with howitzers and Gatling guns, but as the battle raged, they were ordered to wait. The conflict ended very shortly after they got there when the second of the two leaders was shot to death. Billy the Kid escaped and became one of the most famous fugitive outlaws of all time.

Later, there was another history-making event. The Battle of Wounded Knee was fought to stop the escaped Indian chief Big Foot. It was a terrible battle, and many innocent Indians were killed. The Buffalo Soldiers got there almost too late but in just enough time to save the white soldiers from getting killed themselves.

Still later, members of the Buffalo Soldiers' scouting party were surrounded by about fifty Apaches in the mountains near Deming, New Mexico, when Corporal Clifton Greaves used his gun as a club to free his men. Two years later, Apache chief Victorio ambushed them. Several Buffalo Soldiers won the Congressional Medal of Honor for bravery during these skirmishes.

But in the spring of 1898, the Buffalo Soldiers were preparing to fight a new enemy. Of the men who made their way to Cuba, the Buffalo Soldiers were the most highly trained, the most seasoned and the most experienced. And it would soon show.

THE TRIP TO CUBA

Even before the fighting began, there were disasters aplenty. The June heat in Tampa was steamy, suffocating and oppressive. The American soldiers, wearing prickly wool uniforms, were crowded onto the ships. The cavalry units, trained to fight on horseback, were forced to leave their horses behind due to lack of room on the ships. In fact, many men were left behind for the same reason. By the time they arrived in Cuba, many of the soldiers were wretchedly sick. Malaria and yellow fever thinned the ranks even further, and General Wheeler himself was sickened. He led a charge, however, and his men did double takes when, in his weakened state, he yelled, "Come on boys! We've got those Yankees on the run!"

Captain John "Black Jack" Pershing, commander of the Ninth and Tenth Cavalries known as the Buffalo Soldiers, was standing waist-high in a creek when he saw General Wheeler nearby on horseback. Pershing saluted his division commander just as an enemy shell landed between them. As the drenching water from the explosion subsided, Wheeler returned his salute. With that, both men turned back to the battle.

As shells exploded all around, some men ran in panic through the dense jungle. The Spaniards used smokeless powder so that it was impossible to determine where they fired from, while the Americans' guns churned up thick black smoke, giving their positions away. Time and time again, Captain Pershing personally went back into the jungle to find lost troops, guiding and encouraging them back into battle. An officer who watched him described Pershing as "cool as a bowl of cracked ice."

Confusion was everywhere as the men waited for orders, wasting valuable time. Lieutenant Jules Ord of the Seventy-first New York yelled to his men to follow him. The Rough Riders and the Tenth Cavalry joined the Seventy-first as they slowly made their way through the enemy lines. The casualties were horrific, but the Americans pressed onward. The men of the Tenth were divided in the confusion, and some followed Ord's charge up San Juan Hill while others joined Roosevelt's Rough Riders and John Pershing up Kettle Hill.

Lieutenant Ord was the first American to reach the top of San Juan Hill, with the help of the Tenth Cavalry. The brave young man was felled by an enemy bullet, becoming the first American to die on top of San Juan Hill. General Wheeler later remarked that it was the worst fire he had ever seen. The battle claimed half of the officers of the Tenth Cavalry, as well as one out of every five men in the unit. Pershing watched one of his Buffalo Soldiers hold up a wounded Spaniard's head and give him the water out of his own canteen. A wounded officer asked Pershing how badly he was hurt. Pershing told him that he couldn't tell; he then said, "But we whipped them, didn't we?"

The Spaniards lost the battle, and although the war was not yet won, this was a turning point. The Americans, suffering in the intense heat, now had to cope with the onslaught of the rainy season. Malaria and yellow fever were rampant. Pershing and Wheeler were sick. On July 10, American forces began an intense assault on Santiago. The Spaniards finally surrendered on July 17, 1898.

Meanwhile, one month earlier, the town of Huntsville, Alabama, had extended an invitation to the heroes of the Spanish-American War. The "Splendid Little War," as it was called, had ended in mere weeks, but many of the soldiers were still suffering from the effects of malaria and yellow fever. The president of the Huntsville Chamber of Commerce wrote to the secretary of war extolling the virtues of Huntsville's immunity from disease, healthy air and available space. Apparently, the authorities were convinced enough to send Lieutenant Colonel J.A. Cleary in July to see for himself. By August, word had leaked out that regiments from Florida, Georgia, Maryland, Pennsylvania, Indiana, Ohio, New York and Michigan would be sent to Huntsville to recover. It was predicted that Huntsville would have the largest military camp in the entire southeastern United States.

The military encampment was named Camp Wheeler to honor former Confederate general and now U.S. general Joseph Wheeler, but the number of soldiers would far outnumber the number of residents. Within weeks, thousands of soldiers began to arrive. They were weary, war torn, heartsick and homesick. The people of Huntsville welcomed them with open arms. Among them were the men of the Ninth and Tenth Cavalries, the Buffalo Soldiers, who arrived in October.

Though much advancement had been made in the lives of former slaves since the end of the War Between the States, some things had not changed. It was still the segregated South, and so the black and white soldiers were not stationed together in Huntsville. On October 18, 1898, the day of their arrival in Huntsville, members of the Sixteenth Infantry got into a skirmish with members of the Tenth Cavalry. Two Buffalo Soldiers were killed, one provost guardsman was killed and several others were seriously wounded. All had been shot.

Another guest of Huntsville, a member of Troop G, Second Cavalry, served as General John Joseph Coppinger's bodyguard. But this wasn't the first visit by Robert James. He had visited several years before, as a young lad, when his father, famous bank robber Frank James, was tried for robbing the federal payroll near Muscle Shoals.

There were those who were old enough to remember a time when the soldiers in blue were in Huntsville. During the Civil War, the Union army had occupied the town, and bitter feelings of that time still lingered. But this time was different. This time, General Joseph Wheeler himself wore a blue uniform.

A Military Occupation of a Different Kind

Veterans of the Spanish-American War relax in Huntsville. *Photo courtesy Huntsville–Madison County Public Library.*

Members of the Tenth Cavalry pose for a picture in Huntsville. *Photo courtesy Huntsville–Madison County Public Library.*

Tents of the Spanish-American War veterans encamped in and around Huntsville. *Photo courtesy Huntsville–Madison County Public Library.*

General Joe Wheeler was a short, slim man with the demeanor and manners of the stately southern gentleman that he was. His men loved him, and he took care of them. The citizens of Huntsville, ten thousand strong, gathered on December 1 to cheer as he was presented with a fine horse. He changed the name of Camp Wheeler to Camp Albert G. Forse in memory of a man who died during the daring charge up San Juan Hill.

For his role in the Cuban campaign, John Pershing received special recognition from Teddy Roosevelt. He had also come to Huntsville with his men, the members of the Ninth and Tenth Cavalries. Five members of the Tenth Cavalry were awarded the Medal of Honor: Sergeant Major Edward L. Baker Jr., Private Dennis Bell, Private Fitz Lee, Private William H. Thompkins and Private George H. Wanton. In addition, another African American sailor was awarded the Medal of Honor: Private First Class Robert Penn, U.S. Navy.

The people of Huntsville entertained the troops with cotillions and dinners during their stay. Within weeks after Christmas, the veterans of the Spanish-American War began to leave town. In late January 1899, the Tenth Cavalry Band played a song dedicated to their comrades: "The San Juan Trooper's Schottische." On January 28, the Sixty-ninth New York Volunteers returned to their homes, and the Twentieth Cavalry left for Fort Clark, Texas. Huntsville, Alabama, returned to business as usual.

EPILOGUE

John Pershing, who once remarked that he would not make a career of the army because "there won't be a gun fired in the world in a hundred years," was a military genius who trailed Pancho Villa after the Cuban War, before his appointment as leader of the American Expeditionary Force. In 1917, he was

A Military Occupation of a Different Kind

sent to England, on a secret journey, to meet with King George at Buckingham Palace. The task before him was enormous, and at times the enemy seemed to be the Allied commanders he was there to help. Allied commanders had insisted that the American troops be incorporated into theirs, while Pershing insisted that they retain autonomy as American troops under American commanders. Soon after, the Germans overpowered the British Fifth Army in a move that threatened to defeat the Allied army. Pershing sent a letter of support to Marshal Foch, which served to revive the morale of the British and French armies. In part, his message read, "I have come especially to tell you that the American people will be proud to take part in the greatest battle of history."

Pershing commanded over one million American and French soldiers during the attack on the German lines near Verdun in the Meuse-Argonne campaign. The forty-seven-day battle began in late September 1918 and took the Allied army deep into the Argonne Forest. The twisted and mangled limbs of the once-lush forest were left as evidence, along with the thousands of dead soldiers, of the terrible battle. General Pershing was given the title general of the armies of the United States. Although he had received numerous medals, when he walked solemnly behind the caisson that carried the body of the Unknown Soldier to his grave at Arlington, General John "Black Jack" Pershing wore only the Victory Medal, which had been given to every man who served in World War I.

General Joseph Wheeler returned to Alabama and was elected to Congress. At the age of seventy, while visiting his sister in New York, he died of pneumonia. General Wheeler was buried at Arlington National Cemetery, one of the small number of former Confederate veterans interred there.

Theodore Roosevelt was propelled into the White House, largely because of the reputation he earned in the Cuban War.

On November 11, 2009, an impressive statue of a Buffalo Soldier was finally erected in front of the Academy of Arts and Academics in Huntsville,

General Joseph Wheeler on a horse presented to him by the people of Huntsville. *Photo courtesy Huntsville–Madison County Public Library.*

General Joseph Wheeler surrounded by appreciative Huntsville residents. *Photo courtesy Huntsville–Madison County Public Library.*

General Joseph Wheeler observing his men marching in formation around the courthouse square. *Photo courtesy Huntsville–Madison County Public Library.*

Alabama. It took thirteen years to raise the money for the monument and pedestal and finally get it out for all to see. The school—and now the monument— is located on a small hill in northwest Huntsville. Long before the school was there, the small hill was known locally as Cavalry Hill. Although the street that passes in front of the hill is also known as Cavalry Hill, it will now be apparent why, 111 years after the last Buffalo Soldier left town.

The cause of the explosion of the USS *Maine* has always been in question. Recent theorists have studied the facts and have come up with a sound explanation. It is now assumed that the ship was destroyed because of a boiler explosion. Who knows how the course of history would have changed if this had been discovered in time to avoid the Splendid Little War.

Grady Reeves

The Old Man from the Mountain

Once upon a time, a cherub, known as the Littlest Angel, came into Paradise. He was exactly four years, six months, five days, seven hours, and forty-two minutes old when he came to the kingdom of God.

Every Christmas, the mellow voice of Grady Reeves could be heard throughout the Tennessee Valley, reading Charles Tazewell's *The Littlest Angel* to children through the airwaves from radio station WBHP. It was a Christmas tradition he started over half a century ago, and children everywhere tuned in to hear many wonderful holiday stories.

Grady Reeves was born in Carrollton, Georgia, and came to Huntsville, Alabama, in 1947 from Cincinnati, Ohio. In Cincinnati, he had finished his schooling and enrolled in the seminary. His father was furious when he dropped out and took a job doing "the devil's work"—radio. Grady put Rosemary Clooney on the air before her golden voice made her famous worldwide. He was hired in Huntsville by Milton Cummings and Joe Foster to call professional baseball games and high school sports. His career in the Tennessee Valley would far surpass the broadcast of local sports, and it would span more than four decades. Huntsville was in the heart of the Sunny South and was about to explode onto the scene of the worldwide race to space.

Grady's son Robert, who works at WHNT Channel 19 like his father did, recalls a few of the many funny stories from his days of accompanying Grady to local football games. One bitterly cold fall night, Huntsville's Butler High

School was playing against Coffee High School in nearby Florence. The press box was so small that out-of-town reporters had to call the game from the roof. No problem. The local fire department sent their truck out and raised the ladder up to the roof for Grady and Robert, who was a little sprite of about six or seven, to climb up onto the roof.

As the game went on, the night air got colder, and Robert was bundled up in a team member's parka to cut the chill. Their warm breath curled out into the frosty night air. The temperature continued to drop, and Robert was lowered to the ground to sit with the team as he shivered in the icy wind. Grady was too busy calling the game to notice the cold, and in spite of the weather, he was even perspiring because he became so animated in the thrill of the game. It soon got so cold that Grady froze to his chair!

The game was finally over. The Butler High team gathered up its belongings to board the bus for Huntsville. There was a problem for Grady though—during the course of the game, the fire department had received a call to put out a fire and left him stranded on the roof of the press box. The Butler team members stayed with Grady and Robert as long as they could. Though they couldn't help the situation, the boys wanted to keep them company. But the bus was waiting, and the team had to go home to worried parents. Fortunately for Grady and Robert, the fire was finally extinguished, and the ladder truck returned to bring Grady down.

Even though he was very young, Robert became the spotter for Butler's football team and helped Grady in that capacity at all their games. The spotter's job was to identify players by pointing to their names on a list as the play was being made to help the announcer describe the play more thoroughly. It was customary that the opposing team provide a spotter to help Grady relay its information over the radio as well. One night, Butler was playing Cullman High School in Cullman, and Grady explained to the young man representing Cullman's team that they were working with an open microphone. It was live radio, and he needed to be mindful of his language on the air.

The game commenced, and the Rebels were beating the Bearcats like a drum. Suddenly, the Cullman fullback burst through the line and was running hell bent for leather toward the goal line. In his excitement, the young Cullman spotter blurted out, "Look at that sonofabitch go!"

He immediately tried to pull the words back, but it was too late. The two boys, Robert and the Cullman spotter, turned to Grady for some dreaded response. Grady wasn't talking. He had fallen backward off his stool and was lying flat on his back laughing so hard his whole body was shaking. It took a few minutes for him to collect himself, and when he did, he leaned into the microphone. "Ladies and gentlemen, due to technical difficulties, we have been off the air. Our apologies to our listeners."

Grady was broadcasting the play by play of a particularly exciting Alabama football game one night for the University of Alabama. It was a close game, with time winding down, and the Tide was backed up deep in its own territory. Suddenly, the quarterback for Alabama burst through the line headed for pay dirt. Grady was so excited that he lost his composure and began to shout into the microphone.

"And there he goes! Across the forty-, the fifty-, the sixty-, the seventy-yard line!" During those dramatic moments of the game, he leaned out of the window for a closer look, and suddenly the enunciation in his voice changed. Grady's pearly whites had fallen out of his mouth and dropped down into the crowd below.

Although he was torn between diving after them and finishing the game, Grady felt he had no choice but to finish the broadcast sans his front teeth. He waited until the crowd cleared before he went into the stands to retrieve his partial. No reaction was recorded, however, from the startled spectator who was clobbered by Grady's front teeth in the heat of the Tide's victory.

Huntsvillians of a certain age will remember the Holiday House, a restaurant near the present intersection of Governors Drive and the Parkway. On top was a glass booth where Grady would broadcast live for WBHP. It was a popular hangout for teenagers who would park their cars, drive-in style, facing Grady. He would lower a galvanized metal milk bucket down a long rope, and listeners would leave scribbled music requests for him to pull up and play. It was not unusual for Grady to make a typical announcement that "Joe Smith's mother just called and said you need to go home now and finish your homework." In a few minutes, a car would start up, lights would come on and someone would drive off, presumably to finish his homework.

Grady had many friends and, on occasion, a few enemies as well. Shorty Ogle was the head football coach in Decatur and, through some sort of disagreement, took a sudden and intense disliking to Grady. Neither could remember what the falling out was about, but by then, the reason had become irrelevant.

One night, Huntsville's Butler team was in Decatur playing the Red Raider football team. Grady and Robert went to call the game for broadcast on WBHP, but Shorty barred them from the press box. Although it was customary to let the radio announcers in for no charge, Shorty Ogle made sure that Grady bought two tickets and went in with the public. There was only one place they could set up to broadcast, however, thanks to Shorty, and it was their misfortune to sit right next to the Decatur High School band. The band was great but just a tad loud for background on a radio broadcast. To make matters worse, Shorty Ogle instructed the bandleader to start playing music every time Grady opened his mouth. Both men were stubborn as mules and determined to irritate the other, but in the end, the two men buried the hatchet and became great friends.

Over the many years of his professional career, Grady also worked at WFUN, WNDA and WAAY Radio in Huntsville. He also did football play by plays for the University of Alabama in 1956–57 and hired the legendary John Forney as his color man. Forney would become the Tide's play-by-play man for over thirty years. Grady turned to television in 1961, going to work for WAFG-TV Channel 31 as news director and anchor. In 1962, however, he made the mistake of mentioning, on air, his good friend L.D. Wall, who was running for reelection as sheriff. It was a costly mistake, and Grady lost his job at WAFG.

It may have been the best mistake he ever made, however, because not long after Grady found his home at WHNT Channel 19. He was the first employee hired—six months before there was a WHNT—and was one of three who opened the first show on Thanksgiving Day 1963. The nation was still mourning the tragic loss of President John Kennedy, and his death was still in the headlines the week after his assassination. It was a bittersweet broadcast for Grady and the others on that memorable day.

Grady was called on to cover many events that were uncomfortable, to say the least. Channel 19 videographer Dion Hose remembered that he went with Grady to cover a Ku Klux Klan rally one night. Dion had just started his job; he was young and he was very worried. Grady told him that he would be safe with him and everything would be all right. As a young black man, Dion had every reason to be afraid that night, but he soon learned that as long as he was with Grady, he could go anywhere.

Grady's Albertville, Alabama friends, photographer Robert O. Johnson and realtor Fred Taylor, remember that about once a week while he was on the air at WHNT Channel 19, Grady would announce that he was meeting them for lunch that day and give the place and time. If Robert O. and Fred missed the broadcast, someone always called to pass the message on. However, there was no possible way they could enjoy a private lunch together because hundreds of other people who also saw the broadcast wanted to see Grady Reeves in person, get his autograph and maybe even take a picture. But Grady loved it as much as Robert O. and Fred hated it.

Grady Reeves: The Old Man from the Mountain

The owner of one restaurant asked Grady to stop announcing their lunch at his restaurant because he could not handle the hordes of people lined up outside to see Grady.

When Robert O. was in a Birmingham hospital with a serious illness, Grady would announce his progress daily for viewers. Even those who didn't know Robert O. were tuning in for updates on his condition. If Grady missed a day announcing his progress, he got phone calls of inquiry. Everyone was relieved when Robert O. was finally released from the hospital.

Grady, Robert O. and Fred were driving around Boaz one day when a car with those dreaded flashing blue lights appeared in the rearview mirror. Fred, who was driving, pulled over and stopped. The three waited patiently as one of Boaz's finest approached their car for a little chat. Robert O. and Fred thought they could talk their way out of the situation by pointing to the celebrity in their car and asking smugly, "Do you know who *he* is?"

Apparently, the officer was not a fan of morning television, and he even made "the celebrity" ride in the car with him while Fred and Robert O. were instructed to follow the police cruiser to the jail. Fortunately for them, the mayor of Boaz *was* a fan of morning television. When asked about the few hours they spent at the Boaz City Jail, all Robert O. offers by way of explanation is, "Fred was driving."

Grady Reeves carved a niche for himself in the Tennessee Valley. On air, he referred to himself as "the Old Man from the Mountain" while those who knew him called him "Uncle Grady." Every morning, before he drove to the television station, he stopped by Eunice Merrill's restaurant on Andrew Jackson Way to make sure she made it to work safely. He would then go to the station to prepare for his show, *Mornin' Folks*. Until his last show on May 31, 1991, he signed off with the words: "There's always something going on at *Mornin' Folks*, and so am I."

Grady would sign off in the mornings and begin his rounds in the Tennessee Valley. He put an average of fifty thousand miles on his car every year, and he knew people far and wide. He made frequent visits to special-needs children and elderly people in nursing homes and always talked about them on the air. He went every year to the Birdie Thornton School for handicapped children to videotape the kids. In the course of his rounds, he would stop at country stores to get the latest gossip. He also spoke to farmers toiling in their fields, getting their advice and updates so he could report the latest weather or crop news to his viewers.

Keith Lowhorne, former director of news operations at WHNT, recalled that Grady took him under his wing when he started at the station as a high school senior in 1974. Grady would leave notes for Keith, telling him what time to meet him at the station. Wherever they went, Grady always drove and dispensed fatherly advice to the young man along the way. Grady would not tell Keith what kind of adventure he had planned for them, but Keith could count on the two of them doing some serious table grazing wherever they went.

On one occasion, Grady told Keith that they had to empty the trunk of his navy blue Caprice Classic before they could leave. It was no small task, considering the car had been fitted with heavy-duty springs to hold the treasures stored in Grady's trunk. The lid was opened, and out came fishing poles and tackle. They unloaded rain gear, several sets of clothing and video cameras. Shoes, still cameras, film of every kind and golf clubs were dug out as well. Finally, the trunk was empty, and they could begin their odyssey. Grady loved gospel music, and on that day, they had been invited to a country church for a "singing." Still, Keith wondered about the empty car trunk. At the conclusion, everyone gathered for lots of southern comfort food. As Grady and Keith started to leave, they were followed to the car with armloads of food. Fried chicken, potato salad, slaw, corn bread and every kind of dessert imaginable was packed tightly into the trunk. Keith made the ride home balancing a cake and pie in his arms because the trunk was too full.

In the 1980s, Grady spent several days in Huntsville Hospital. A bus pulled up into the parking lot, and several young men with longish hair hopped off and went inside to call on Grady. They walked the halls looking for his room, and pretty soon, the small entourage began to pick up strays and, finally, a crowd. They got to Grady's room but were soon asked to leave by concerned nurses because of the commotion their presence was beginning to cause. The friendly boys from Fort Payne left after paying their respects to Grady. Those friendly boys were, of course, the country singing sensation that goes by the name Alabama.

One of the charities Grady supported wholeheartedly was the Muscular Dystrophy Association. He was the original host of the local Jerry Lewis MDA Telethon on WHNT, a tradition he upheld for ten years before turning it over to his son, Robert, and WHNT anchor Jerry Hayes. In those days, the hosts worked twenty-four hours straight, asking viewers to pledge money for continued research. The long hours and emotional turmoil of losing children to MD began to take a physical toll on him. In 1989, he emceed his last telethon. To this day, people still call in pledges to the annual Muscular Dystrophy Telethon in Grady's memory. Robert has carried on

Grady's tradition for over twenty-nine years as Channel 19 continues to host the annual Labor Day Telethon, a fundraiser for research money to find a cure for muscular dystrophy.

Robert co-hosted *Mornin' Folks* with his father for the last ten years, but the original format of the show ended with Grady's retirement. Grady's health was questionable at best, and he died in August 1991.

Many newcomers to the area tuned in to watch Grady on television only to wonder what kind of hick place they had moved to. One woman had just moved to Huntsville from somewhere out West and tuned in to hear him talk about Aunt Eunice's ham biscuits and tell Hazel Buttram at Buttram's Crossroads to put the big pot and the little pot on the stove for him 'cause he was coming to visit that day. She wondered to herself what kind of backward town she had come to live in but found herself tuning in again the next day, and the next day too, because she felt somehow welcomed into the show.

After Grady's death, Robert made an appearance at the WHNT-sponsored Senior Expo. An elderly black woman approached Robert and told a story about the time she met Grady years ago. As a small child, she was standing outside a store in Lawrence County on a hot summer day. Grady asked her what was wrong, and she told him she wanted an ice cream cone but couldn't go into the store because black people were not allowed inside. It broke Grady's heart, and he promptly went inside and bought ice cream for the little girl, as well as the other children with her. It was an act of kindness she would never forget.

Grady did not grasp the influence he had on his viewers in the Tennessee Valley. Before his death in 1991 at the age of sixty-eight, he predicted that he would be forgotten a year after his death. As long as there is even one person alive who has ever listened to him through radio or watched him on television, Grady Reeves will be remembered.

Conspiracy!

Abraham Lincoln, the sixteenth president of the United States, was dead. John Wilkes Booth, a popular actor at Ford's Theatre, had shot him. The country was in turmoil, but no one knew yet if Lincoln's death was a conspiracy or the act of a lone rabid Confederate. The army immediately started rounding up anyone with whom Booth was known to have had contact. The list of accused co-conspirators grew by the hour, and one of the men on that list was well known to the people of Huntsville, Alabama. The name Clement Clay would soon be known all over the world.

Booth had fled from Ford's Theatre on horseback, riding out of Washington past the sentry at the Navy Yard Bridge under the cover of darkness. He was in terrible agony; he had broken his leg as he fell from the balcony after mortally wounding the president. He planned to rendezvous with several others but met only David Herold, a co-conspirator who was assigned the duty of leading Lewis Powell out of Washington after he murdered Secretary of State William H. Seward. Herold was outside the Seward home during the assassination attempt but had bolted when he heard screams inside, leaving Lewis Powell to fend for himself.

Booth and Herold met up at Surratt's Tavern, gathered up some supplies and rode out. At about 4:00 a.m., the two arrived at the home of Dr. Samuel Mudd. Although the doctor had met Booth before, Booth tried to conceal his identity, and Dr. Mudd, with no knowledge of what had transpired just a few hours earlier, went along with it and pretended not to know him. Mudd set Booth's broken leg, and the two fugitives slept as the weariness washed over them.

In the early afternoon, they went to Zekiah Swamp. Colonel Samuel Cox provided food for them for the next four days as they waited in the swamp for a chance to escape. On April 20, the two men made their way across the Potomac River in a stolen skiff but drifted north instead of south and ended up in Maryland instead of Virginia. The next night, with precious time working against them, they managed to get to Virginia. For the next several days, Booth and Herold went from one place to another seeking refuge while the frenzied manhunt for them crept ever closer.

On April 24, the two men crossed the Rappahannock River and, with the help of a guide, made their way to the Garrett Farm near Port Royal, Virginia. Booth had been in extreme pain the entire time, and understandably, his condition impeded their flight. But soon that would not matter. Booth had seemed like a pleasant enough guest at the Garrett household, but the family began to be suspicious of the excuse he made up to explain his injury and the extreme paranoia whenever a stranger ventured near. They had no idea who he was, but they wanted no more of him. On the evening of April 25, John Garrett, son of the owner, Richard Garrett, ordered them out of the house. The two men were appalled at his lack of hospitality. After all, they had slept on beds the night before, inside the house. Garrett stood firm, and though he was worried because Booth still had a pistol holstered on his hip, Garrett agreed to let them sleep in the tobacco barn. At 9:00 p.m., the visitors went to sleep on their beds of hay.

John Garrett and his brother, William, worried about the safety of the family and their farm horses. The brothers decided to sleep outside that night in case the two fugitives did something drastic. Very quietly, they locked the door of the barn from the outside. Booth and Herold were now their prisoners.

On the early morning of April 26, the Sixteenth New York Cavalry, consisting of twenty-five men, entered the Garrett household shortly after 1:00 a.m. and demanded to know where Booth and Herold were. They threatened to string up the elderly Richard Garrett, who was understandably confused. John Garrett came forward and offered to tell where the fugitives were, but instead of appreciation for his cooperation, a soldier grabbed him roughly and thrust a revolver against his temple.

As the dogs barked in alarm, the tobacco shed was surrounded, but Booth and Herold were already awake. They had heard the horses' hooves in the distance and tried to escape through the door, only to find it locked from the outside. David Herold tried to kick out a board in the back of the barn, but the nails were solid. Booth tried to kick too, but in his condition, his attempt was feeble and unproductive.

Conspiracy!

Lieutenant Luther Baker informed John Garrett that he would be sent inside the barn, alone and unarmed, to take the weapons from the two prisoners. When Garrett resisted, explaining that Booth was armed and reminding Baker that he was not, Baker threatened to burn down all of the buildings on the farm, including the house. It was *not* a request.

Garrett went inside, but when Booth reached for his revolver, he turned and ran out the door. Lieutenant Baker yelled to Booth that he had to surrender or he would burn the barn down. It was now 2:30 a.m. With the knowledge that they were about to be captured, dead or alive, the two men inside began to argue.

"You don't choose to give yourself up, let me go out and give myself up," Herold told Booth. But Booth threatened to shoot him if he did. The men outside warned them that the barn would be set ablaze in fifteen minutes. Booth told Herold to go. He stumbled outside to soldiers who immediately grabbed him. Dry pine needles were piled near the wall of the barn and a lit "Lucifer stick" was dropped into the pile.

Rising flames licked the dry wooden walls and quickly reached into the barn. The soldiers peered in through the boards, and they could see Booth clearly through the firelight. Although orders were that he was to be taken alive, Sergeant Boston Corbett aimed with his revolver through the cracks of the boards. One account says that he was aiming for Booth's arm, but Booth moved, and the bullet found its mark through his neck, paralyzing him instantly. Corbett later claimed that divine providence had directed him to fire his weapon.

Booth dropped his weapon and fell to his knees. Several men rushed in and grabbed him before he could fall to the ground. He was taken out and placed under a nearby tree as the flames consumed the barn. Booth was then carried to the porch of the Garrett home and a pillow was placed under his head. He was in physical misery, unable to move, unable to find relief as the soldiers repositioned him at his direction. He could not cough, he could not swallow and he begged for someone to kill him. But Secretary of War Edwin Stanton wanted him alive.

The Garrett men worked feverishly to contain the fire at the barn, but it was too far gone.

"Tell Mother I die for my country," Booth whispered as the sun began to rise. His breathing was inconsistent, he gasped a few times, his throat was swollen and his heartbeats were irregular. "My hands," he said. Someone raised Booth's hands for him to look, and then he spoke his last words, "Useless, useless." He gasped again, and his body shuddered. After two hours of most agonizing pain, the assassin died of asphyxia.

At 8:30 a.m., the body of John Wilkes Booth was sewn into a horse blanket, put onto a stretcher and carried in a wagon to Belle Plain. There it was put onto the deck of the steamer *John S. Ide* and taken to Alexandria. The body was then placed on a tugboat and carried to Washington Navy Yard, where it was placed on the *Montauk*. At 1:45 a.m. on April 27, the autopsy, performed by Surgeon General Joseph K. Barnes and Dr. Joseph J. Woodward, began.

Booth's body had endured much physical abuse in the previous twelve days. He looked haggard; he was unshaven, and he barely resembled the handsome actor from two weeks earlier. His dentist looked inside his mouth to examine his teeth and confirmed that it was Booth. His surgeon, who had removed a tumor from Booth's neck, also identified him. Finally, his friends knew him to have a homemade tattoo on his left hand between his thumb and forefinger that bore his initials: J.W.B.

The assassin's body was taken to the Old Penitentiary on Washington Arsenal (now Fort Lesley McNair) and was buried under the floor of a cell. It was covered with a stone slab.

Booth's death did not do much to relieve the anger of the American public. The hue and cry was for justice to be served, no matter who was involved in the conspiracy. Mary Surratt, the owner of the tavern where Booth and Herold had stopped for guns and supplies, had been arrested on April 17 and taken to the Old Capitol Prison. She was later taken to Washington Arsenal Penitentiary. Others named and arrested as co-conspirators were Lewis Powell, who had tried to murder William Seward; George Atzerodt, who was supposed to have killed Vice President Andrew Johnson but got drunk instead; David Herold, who helped Booth in his attempt to escape; Michael O'Laughlin; Edward Spangler; Samuel Arnold; and Samuel Mudd. Mary's son, John, a Confederate courier and friend of Booth's, was wanted by the authorities but could not be found. The trial for all eight named as co-conspirators began on May 12.

CONFEDERATE LEADERS ARRESTED

In the meantime, another drama was unfolding farther south. Confederate president Jefferson Davis and his cabinet had evacuated Richmond, Virginia, the Confederate headquarters, on April 2. While attending church services, Davis received a telegram from General Robert E. Lee urging him to leave at once. President Davis fled to Danville, then to Greensboro, North Carolina, and on to Charlotte. Davis knew the war was over when he saw the articles of surrender agreed upon by U.S. general W.T. Sherman and Confederate general J.E. Johnston. Yet he still clung to the hope of resurrecting the cause of the Confederacy. The last cabinet meeting was held on April 26 in Charlotte.

Clement C. Clay attended the last cabinet meeting in Charlotte and headed south with his wife, Virginia. The Huntsville native had announced Alabama's secession from the Union at the U.S. Senate meeting back on January 21, 1861. He was offered the job as secretary of war for the Confederacy but turned it down, suggesting another Huntsville native, Leroy Pope Walker, for the position. Clay became a member of the Confederate Congress, and his picture graced the Confederate one-dollar bill. While the Clays waited in LaGrange, Georgia, Virginia Clay went to the train station to find out what currency they would accept for passage to Macon. The conductor informed her that Macon had surrendered to the Federals and Atlanta was already under their control. Virginia Clay asked the conductor if there was any other news about the warrant for President Jefferson Davis's arrest. The conductor, who had no idea who she was, told her that there was a $100,000 reward for the capture of Clement Clay of Alabama. (It was actually only $25,000, but with each telling, the amount increased.)

Virginia hurried back to the house where she and her husband were staying to tell him the horrible news. It was no use to run. They rode to Atlanta to surrender and, under Federal guard, rode on to Macon. Clay learned that he was wanted for his part in the conspiracy to murder the president. A rumor had been circulated that Clay had once met with Booth in Canada to discuss an assassination plot. Clay was taken into custody, and his wife was given permission to accompany him. Surely, the couple thought, Clay would be released when the truth was finally told.

Days earlier, President Davis had asked that General Joseph "Fightin' Joe" Wheeler and General Wade Hampton protect him while he reconstructed the Confederate government.

"I can do this, Mr. President," Wheeler said. "That is, gather from my command a body of new men who will stand by you in a new enterprise." But Wheeler cautioned Davis that the majority of the soldiers considered the war over and no longer felt allegiance to the Southern cause. They were sick of it all and wanted simply to go home.

Wheeler returned to his men, announced his decision to follow President Davis and asked for volunteers. He was surprised that there was no show of emotion—no cheering, no rally cry, no joy in any form—but in spite of their weariness, six hundred men agreed to go with their commander.

Wheeler and his men arrived in Yorkville, South Carolina, to pay a visit to General Hampton. Only thirty of Hampton's men volunteered to keep fighting, but as they made their way south, one by one, the men began to peel off and head back to their homes. By the time General Hampton neared his home in South Carolina, only one of his men remained, General Henry B. McClellan. When they reached the Peedee River, even General McClellan decided that he had had enough.

General Wheeler and his men continued on to rendezvous with Jefferson Davis in Georgia, without Hampton or his reinforcements. But President Davis was beginning to see the truth of the situation, and he let his own troops go home so he could decide where to go next. According to some sources, his intention was to meet up with Kirby Smith in Texas to regroup, while another possible plan was to head to Florida. But his destiny was not the one he had chosen. On the early morning of May 10, 1865, Jefferson Davis, along with members of his family and that of his wife, was captured near Irwinville, Georgia, by Colonel Benjamin D. Pritchard and the Fourth Michigan Cavalry.

General Wheeler and the few who were left of his six hundred men were surrounded in the Georgia pine forests and thickets. Wheeler sent scouts into the enemy camps to find out what they could, but they were arrested. They escaped and returned to General Wheeler, but it was clear that Federal forces were not far behind. General Wheeler and his men fled through the darkness and stopped at daylight to set up camp in a clearing. They gave some money to a black man to bring them food, which he did, but on his way out, he was intercepted by Federal troops, who captured Wheeler and his men while they slept.

General Joseph Wheeler was taken to Athens, Georgia, and then sent on to Augusta, where he would be reunited with Jefferson Davis and his wife and children; Vice President Alexander Stephens; Huntsville native Clement Clay and his wife, Virginia; former Governor Francis Lubbock of Texas; and others.

The prisoners were placed on a train headed toward Augusta. It was a horrible trip. Davis, Stephens and Clay were extremely sick, and every town they passed had crowds trying to get a glimpse of the Federal prisoners.

At one town, a Union soldier assigned to guard the prisoners called out to the Southern crowd, "Hey Johnny Reb! We've got your president!"

"And the devil's got yours!" was the angry reply.

The train stopped in Augusta, and the whole city was in chaos. General Wheeler was already there. It was Wheeler's hometown, and it must have been especially sad for his father and sisters, who were there to see their war hero, now in bondage and bound for prison, possibly even execution.

In Augusta, the prisoners were placed on the tugboat *William P. Clyde* with the *Tuscarora* as their escort, guns pointed at the tugboat full of prisoners and sailors ready to fire. Jefferson Davis was confined below deck, suffering from a painful headache. On the deck above, General Joseph Wheeler was talking to Virginia Clay. As he gazed out into the distance, he leaned innocently against the guardrail. A Union officer slapped him with the blade of his sword and snarled, "It is against the rule to lean on the guardrail!"

Joseph Wheeler, ever the Southern gentleman, touched his hat and replied, "I did not know the rule, sir, or I would not have infringed it."

As the officer walked away, Mrs. Clay, who was not known for her restraint, told him that she was in awe of his self-control and courtesy. "Had I been a man, that Yankee would have been exploring the bottom of the Savannah River, or I, one."

At Savannah, the entire party was moved onto a larger steamer to begin the journey north. Varina Davis, Jefferson Davis's wife, was struggling to take care of her sick husband, all the while holding a baby in her arms. General Wheeler offered to take the baby, and for hours on end, he walked the deck with baby Winnie Davis in his arms while she tugged at his beard.

On May 19, the steamer arrived at Fort Monroe and dropped anchor, awaiting further orders. On May 21, General Wheeler and his staff boarded another ship headed to Fort Delaware. As they had come to suspect, Clement Clay and Jefferson Davis would be imprisoned at Fort Monroe (also known as Fortress Monroe) in Hampton. Ironically, slaves had known it as the "Freedom Fortress" because, by order of Benjamin Butler, any slave who reached the fort would be freed.

As the two men said their goodbyes to their families and disappeared, a soldier looked down at Davis's son and said, "Don't cry Jeff. They ain't going to hang your pa!" Clement Clay's wife handed him a volume of *Jay's Family Prayers* as they parted company. Inside the front cover, she had written her desperate thoughts: "My dear husband, can I not see you? Will not General Miles permit me to visit you once under guard? If not, where am I to go and when? Farewell and may God bless you. Your wife." Inside the back cover, she wrote another message: "Oh my God. Into Thy hands I command my precious husband at sea. 20th May." Under her handwriting, another ominous message was scribbled: "2 O'Clock, 10 minutes, entered prison at Fort Monroe on Monday May 22/65."

The wives were left on the boat, wondering what was next for them. They were strip-searched by two women to ensure they had no important papers in their clothing. "Oh Ginny, what humiliation!" Varina Davis said.

"I would die before they should see me shed tears!" Virginia said defiantly.

"You haven't four little children about you," Varina answered. The ladies and children were returned to Savannah and left to fend for themselves.

Over the next few weeks, the newspapers printed "opinions of the press"—suggestions on what to do with the new prisoners. One said, "We hope soon to see the bodies of these two arch traitors, Davis and Clay, dangling and blackening in the wind and rain!"

On June 29, the military commission met in a secret session to determine the fate of the eight co-conspirators whose trial had taken seven weeks to complete. The next day, it announced its decision: David Herold, George Atzerodt, Lewis Payne and Mary Surratt would hang by the neck until dead. Michael O'Laughlin, Samuel Arnold and Dr. Samuel Mudd were sentenced to hard labor for life. Edward Spangler was sentenced to hard labor for six years.

No one expected Mary Surratt to hang. The jury had recommended leniency because of her age and sex, but President Johnson refused to let her go, saying that she was the one who "kept the nest that hatched the egg."

On July 7, 1865, a huge crowd assembled to watch the hanging. They surrounded the gallows that had been prepared at the Old Arsenal Building. Because there were so many who wanted to catch a glimpse of the historic moment, only those who had been issued tickets could stand in the courtyard. At 1:26 p.m., the three men and one woman were led up the stairs. Hoods were placed over their heads and nooses around their necks. George Atzerodt said, "May we meet in another world. God take me now," and then the trapdoors were sprung, four ropes snapped taut and four bodies dangled in the stifling hot air.

Jefferson Davis and Huntsville's Clement Clay heard the news while waiting in their cells. They wondered if they were next.

Legacy of an Assassination

Confederate president Jefferson Davis and former member of his Confederate Congress Clement C. Clay were kept in separate cells, in solitary confinement, at Fortress Monroe, Virginia. They had been accused of plotting to assassinate President Lincoln, but no charges had formally been brought against them. Rumors flew across the country that Jeff Davis had been apprehended while dressed in women's clothing, and silly cartoons of him in drag were circulated in newspapers. In truth, he had grabbed a shawl to put over his shoulders, and although he thought it was his own shawl, it belonged to his wife.

Clement Claiborne Clay, a native of Huntsville, Alabama, had grown up in privilege as the son of Alabama's eighth governor. Clement was an attorney and, like his father, had entered politics. He had the dubious distinction of announcing Alabama's secession from the Union in January 1861 and took his place in the newly formed Confederate Congress. While the Union soldiers occupied Huntsville, General Ormsby Mitchel's family was living, uninvited to say the least, in the Clay household. Mitchel's daughter was known to ride about town on Virginia's mare, wearing Virginia's green riding habit. On one such stroll about town, a girl of about fourteen or so yelled angrily at the intruder, "Get off of Ginnie's mare!" Later that day, the brother of the teenager was arrested under a trumped-up charge.

Clay had lived for a time in Richmond as a member of the Confederate Congress, but when his term was up, he went to Canada in an attempt to help relieve his aggravating asthma condition. But now it was all over; Robert E. Lee had surrendered, and President Lincoln had been assassinated. When Clay found that a reward was offered for his capture, he did the honorable thing by turning himself in to authorities. After all, he was innocent of the charges of conspiracy to assassinate the president, and he had every reason to believe that when the mistake was discovered, he would be released and sent home—or so he thought. But fate is not always aligned with truth. On May 22, 1865, he entered his new home in solitary confinement. His wife, Virginia, begged him to run, but in the end, she went with him as far as the prison.

Virginia Clay returned to Huntsville to find her husband's parents in poor health and failing daily from the stress of the war and their son's imprisonment. Around Huntsville, little cotton had been planted in the countryside, and the horrendous tax on cotton had been imposed to further devastate the impoverished population. Confusion was everywhere—everyone was in charge, yet no one was in charge. The Clays' home had been taken over by the Freedman's Bureau, and the former governor and his wife were confined to a

Clement C. Clay. *Photo courtesy Huntsville–Madison County Public Library.*

Confederate president Jefferson Davis and Confederate congressman Clement C. Clay.
Photo courtesy Huntsville–Madison County Public Library.

Virginia Clay. *Photo courtesy Huntsville–Madison County Public Library.*

small apartment within it. Their son, J. Withers Clay, had been sick but had no money to pay the medical director, Dr. French, who generously donated his services. J. Withers Clay's wife, Mary, sent chamomile blossoms as a token of appreciation to the doctor with the note, "These chamomile blossoms are like the Southern ladies—the more they are bruised and oppressed the sweeter and stronger they grow." Virginia took the words to heart and used them to fortify her strength.

With an uncertain future before them, Clement Clay and Jefferson Davis waited with fear and worry in their prison cells. Their repeated requests to speak with U.S. general Henry W. Halleck were denied, and they wondered if they, too, would swing by the neck until dead as the four accused of plotting Lincoln's assassination had done. Their prison cells were heavily fortified with bars on the windows and doors. At least five guards were assigned to each prisoner, as well as several other sentries and general officers stationed around the building doors. They were checked on every fifteen minutes, and a lamp was kept burning at all times inside their rooms. Other sentries watched from atop a parapet, more from across the moat and still others kept the vicinity of the casemate off-limits. Although he was in precarious health, irons were placed on Jefferson Davis's ankles. When the wooden doors were replaced with locked doors of iron bars, the irons and chains were removed from the Confederate president.

As the country waited to find out what would happen to these two men, others were concerned about the wives and families of Clay and Davis. Fannie Hundley of Limestone County, Alabama, had lost her husband in the Civil War, but she would not forget others who had suffered as well. In her ledger, she recorded a six-dollar donation to Varina Davis while Jefferson Davis languished in his cell.

Throughout his imprisonment, Clement C. Clay kept his small prayer book ever close. His wife had given him *Jay's Family Prayers* for much-needed inspiration. He even used it as a journal, writing his notes in tiny letters near the spine of the book. This book, now in possession of the Huntsville–Madison County Library Archives, contains glimpses into Clay's fragile mind:

> *Aug 3/65* NY Herald *brought to me—1ˢᵗ newspaper since I entered prison.*
> *Slept last night (Sept. 14/65) about 6 hours without waking—more than*
> *I have any night during my 116 nights in this prison. This comes from*
> *the removal of guards.*

Oct. 2: Mr. D[avis] moved to Carroll Hall—room fitted as a prison for him.

Oct. 13—A negro hung today—saw the military and heard the music— heard the voice of Mrs. Bickley this evening, first time heard woman's voice since coming in here.

Nov. 4/65: Put on my flannel shirt—cold…I am walking out without guard with Capt. Beck U.S.A.—came near fainting.

Jefferson Davis was examined by surgeon G.E. Cooper, and his report to President Andrew Johnson contained disturbing information:

He is considerably emaciated…he has but little muscular strength. He is quite weak and debilitated…his nervous system is greatly deranged…slight noises, which are scarcely perceptible to a man in robust health, cause him much pain…want of sleep has been a great and almost principal cause of his nervous excitability…Should he be attacked with any of the severe forms of disease to which the Tidewater region of Virginia is subject, I, with reason, fear the result.

The outcry was immediate, especially in the North. Newspapers called for more humane treatment and help for his shameful physical and mental condition. Still, both men felt eyes upon them, night and day, and were awakened every two hours as the sentries were replaced; they remained in their damp, "living tomb," as Clay referred to it, not allowed to speak to anyone or even shake hands with the guards. Privileged visitors who came to the prison were escorted to peer inside the cells at the two men, as if they were caged animals in a zoo. In his first letter to his wife, Clay wrote, "If you ever get my [Jay's] prayer-book, you will see scratched with a pencil, borrowed for the occasion, such items in my monotonous prison life as I felt worth recording." Clay was writing to Virginia as if he would never see her again.

Back in Huntsville, Virginia spent the remaining summer and early fall wondering what to do next. Never one to sit quietly and let nature take its course, she embarked on a campaign to free her husband from prison. In mid-November, she left Huntsville, escorted by Major W.H. Echols of Huntsville, who planned a trip to Washington to register a patent. They began their journey and were surprised to find aid in the form of many Southern sympathizers who refused payment for their services. Virginia wrote letters home of the changing living conditions as they proceeded north. Their land, which had not been so devastated as the South, was still full of good fruits, plentiful goods and unscorched ground.

Upon their arrival in Washington, Virginia Clay personally asked President Andrew Johnson for help in securing her husband's freedom. He rather rudely told her that the decision was Secretary of War Edwin Stanton's. Virginia made an appointment with Edwin Stanton, but he assured her that he was neither the judge nor the accuser of Clay and could not help. She found out later that he had thwarted all attempts to have him released. She then sought General Ulysses Grant, who graciously offered to write a letter in support of her request to the president. Still, nothing happened. Virginia kept repeated appointments to meet with the president to ask for her husband's release or, at the very least, a copy of the charges against him so she could prepare for his defense should he go to trial.

Eventually, she obtained a copy of the charges against her husband. She was appalled to find that a man named G.J. Hyams, alias Harris, had claimed to have proof that Clay had conspired with John Surratt while in Canada to assassinate President Lincoln. (Hyams would later admit that he had perjured himself to the Judiciary Committee.) It was now well into December, and she worked daily to find the right help. Clay wrote that month, "Dec. 17/65 Dear father's birthday—now 76 if living. May God grant he may be till I see him in the flesh."

By late December, with news that her mother-in-law was on the verge of death, Virginia once again pleaded with President Johnson to parole her husband in order to see his mother one last time. Instead, the president gave her written permission to see Clement Clay in prison. On board the New Line steamer *George Leary*, she found the utmost sympathy and kindness from the ship's captain, a Maine native named S. Blakeman. He even issued a pass to her for free rooms and meals "to all points as she wishes." Captain Blakeman personally saw to it that Virginia ate to keep her strength up and invited her to eat with him at the captain's table.

But upon the early morning arrival at the office of General Miles, Virginia found herself once again up against a brick wall. By late afternoon, with the help of Dr. Henry Vogell, who barked, "Miles, for God's sake, let the woman go to her husband!" she was finally allowed to see Clement Clay as the evening shadows fell on the dreary walls of the prison. Dr. Vogell would secretly become another of Virginia's allies. Clay's scribbling that month reads, "Jan. 4/66 Oh sinful creature—Lord have mercy on me."

Virginia Clay wrote and visited anyone who would listen to her. She continued her pleadings with President Johnson. Senator Wilson, vice president of the United States, even wrote a letter supporting the release or parole of Clay. Finally, on April 17, 1866, President Johnson issued an order for his release, carefully worded so as not to imply that he had issued it, against the wishes of Secretary of War Stanton. But it was too late for Clay's mother in Huntsville. She had died in early January. Clement Clay was released the next day and, without stopping to visit friends along the way, returned as quickly as he could to Alabama to see his dying father. He made it with a few weeks to spare.

Jefferson Davis was finally released the following year. Both had been officially paroled but were never brought to trial. Revenge against the South would be exacted through Reconstruction. But the lives of the many people who were personally touched by the assassination of President Lincoln would never be the same.

AFTERMATH

In 1867, John Wilkes Booth's body was dug up at the Old Penitentiary at Washington Arsenal and reburied in the locked storeroom in Warehouse 1, now Fort Leslie McNair. In 1869, it was exhumed yet again and handed over to Booth's family, who buried him in the family plot at Green Mount Cemetery in Baltimore. His grave remains unmarked.

A total of $104,999.60 in reward money was given to a number of men who were connected to the capture of the conspirators. Richard Garrett, who owned the farm where Booth was killed, put in a claim for $4,691 to the U.S. government for the loss of his tobacco barn, the contents and the corn and hay eaten by the horses of the Sixteenth New York. His claim was denied. Boston Corbett, who had fired the fatal bullet at Booth, received $1,653.84 for his part and became famous as "Lincoln's Avenger." He turned down an offer of $1,000 for his Colt revolver. It was stolen shortly thereafter. Corbett remained famous for some time. He received fan mail and many requests to take his picture, but when the fanfare died down, he became an assistant doorkeeper at the Kansas House of Representatives. In 1887, he held the legislature hostage with his revolver. No one was killed, but when he was forced to surrender, he was sent to an asylum for the insane in Topeka. He escaped the next year and was not heard from again. The mysterious actions of the man who said that providence had guided his hand to shoot Booth were of no surprise to people who knew him. As a young man, he had castrated himself.

Legacy of an Assassination

Dr. Samuel Mudd, Samuel Arnold and Michael O'Laughlin were tried and sentenced to a lifetime of hard labor at Albany Penitentiary in New York. Ned Spangler was sentenced to six years, but all four men were sent by Edwin Stanton to Dry Tortugas Prison off of Key West, Florida. A yellow fever epidemic hit the prison in 1867, taking the prison doctor as one of its many victims. Dr. Mudd volunteered to take the doctor's place, and as such, he saved the lives of many of the sick prisoners and employees. Prison officials appealed to authorities for Dr. Mudd's pardon. On February 8, 1869, President Andrew Johnson pardoned Dr. Mudd, Samuel Arnold and Ned Spangler. Michael O'Laughlin had already died in prison during the yellow fever epidemic. Ned Spangler, terminally ill with tuberculosis, went to live with Dr. Mudd until his death in 1875 at age forty. He was buried at Saint Peter's Cemetery in Charles County, Maryland. Dr. Mudd died in 1883 at age fifty but admitted before his death that he knew he had treated John Wilkes Booth, though of course he had not known what had transpired only hours before. He was buried at Saint Mary Cemetery in La Plata, Maryland. A 1936 movie, *The Prisoner of Shark Island*, was made about him. Samuel Arnold died in 1906 at age seventy-two and was buried at Green Mount Cemetery in Baltimore. Michael O'Laughlin was buried at the prison where he died, but his remains were later turned over to his mother for burial at the Green Mount Cemetery. He was twenty-seven at the time of his death.

Henry Rathbone and Clara Harris, who had been guests of the Lincolns at Ford's Theatre, married in 1867. As a government consul, Rathbone took his family to live in Germany. But eighteen years later, Rathbone, who had not been quite right since the night of the assassination, shot his wife and then stabbed her to death for paying too much attention to their three children. When the authorities were summoned to their home on the evening of December 23, 1883, Rathbone stood over Clara and said, "Who could have done this to my lovely bride?" He died in an insane asylum in 1911 at age seventy-four. He was buried in Hannover, Germany, but his remains were disposed of years later when there had been no contact from his family regarding his grave site.

Laura Keene, the actress who starred in the April 14 performance and who cradled President Lincoln's head in her lap as he lay dying, achieved more fame on that night alone than in her whole lifetime. The spring floral dress that she wore, covered with splotches of the president's blood and brain matter, was saved simply because of the morbidity attached to it. It eventually became a burden to her, perhaps for the memories, or maybe because of the number of people who wished to see it and touch it. Today, only a few swatches of it have survived. Laura, who was born in England, died at age forty-seven.

John T. Ford, owner of Ford's Theatre, was arrested by order of Edwin Stanton and accused of being a conspirator in the plot to kill the president. After more than a month, he was finally released, and on the day that the four Lincoln conspirators were hanged, he was given possession of Ford's Theatre once again. Although several people had already threatened to burn it down, he planned to reopen it as a theatre, but public outcry was too much. Ford was paid $100,000 for the building, and Stanton ordered the inside gutted at a cost of $28,500. It became a three-floor office building to house the War Department's records. On June 9, 1893, the top floor collapsed from the weight of papers, and it crushed the floors beneath it, killing twenty-two people and injuring sixty-eight. Today, it is a museum maintained by the National Park Service, and the theatre has been restored to the way it looked on the night of April 14, 1865. The same portrait of George Washington, which was nailed between the buntings in front of the presidential box, is once again in front of that box. John Ford died in 1894.

William Petersen, the man who owned the boardinghouse where the president drew his last breath, committed suicide in 1871 in front of the Smithsonian Museum. He was sixty-one. Petersen is buried at Prospect Hill Cemetery in Washington, D.C.

Tad Lincoln, son of Abraham and Mary Lincoln, died in 1871 at age eighteen. He was the third of the three sons who died young. Mary, who had never been very stable, mentally or emotionally, was committed to an asylum for the insane. She was released, though she was never "normal." She died at age sixty-four in 1882 in the same house she had been married in forty years earlier. Her death was attributed to a stroke.

Robert Todd Lincoln was secretary of war under President James Garfield. In 1881, he was invited to take a trip with Garfield and was on his way to the train station to meet him. Just as he arrived, President Garfield was shot. Garfield subsequently died of his wounds. Twenty years later, in 1901, Robert was invited to join President William McKinley at the Pan-Am Exposition in Buffalo, New York. As he arrived, President McKinley was mortally wounded by a gunman. Lincoln was also with New York mayor William Gaynor when he was shot on August 9, 1910. Lincoln refused after that to be in the physical company of another U.S. president. Lincoln died at age eighty-three in 1926. He is buried at Arlington National Cemetery, the only one of his family not buried at the Lincoln family plot in Springfield, Illinois. Today, there are no living direct heirs to President Lincoln. As an interesting side note, David Todd, Confederate veteran and brother of Mary Todd Lincoln, died in Huntsville, Alabama, shortly after the Civil War and is buried at Maple Hill Cemetery.

Conspirator Lewis Powell, who had been hanged for his part in the crime, had been buried at the old arsenal but was dug up in 1869 and reburied at Holmead Cemetery in Washington. Somehow, his head ended up at the Smithsonian Institution. It was discovered in 1993, taken to Florida and buried on November 11, 1994. His body has not been found.

Conspirator Mary Surratt was buried in the shallow grave next to the fence at the old arsenal along with the other three conspirators. After their hanging, they had been stripped naked and wrapped in sheets, their clothing given to charity and pieces of their hair and bits of rope sold to souvenir hunters. At the request of her daughter, Anna, Mary was reinterred four years later at Mount Olivet Cemetery in Washington. Her home, now a part of Chinatown, was most recently a Chinese restaurant.

Conspirator David Herold, twenty-three at the time of his execution by hanging, was buried in the shallow grave near the gallows but was dug up in February 1869 for reburial at the Congressional Cemetery. The undertaker described the condition of his temporary grave: the lid had fallen in, and no flesh was left on his skeleton. All of the conspirators had a glass vial holding a piece of paper with their name written on it. The vial was given to Herold's mother, and his body was placed in a walnut coffin and buried in the family plot in an unmarked grave.

Conspirator George Atzerodt, who was supposed to assassinate Vice President Andrew Johnson, was removed to Glenwood Cemetery in Washington and later to St. Paul's in Baltimore. He is buried in a grave under a headstone with the name Gottlieb Taubert.

General Joseph "Fightin' Joe" Wheeler, who had been captured and imprisoned at Fort Delaware, barely survived the horrible diseases that took so many lives in the prison. He was paroled in late July and returned to Augusta, first stopping in Courtland, Alabama, at the home of widow Daniella Jones Sherrod. He later married the young woman and eventually made his home in Courtland. He spent the next few years in politics, serving in Congress. During the Spanish-American War, Wheeler fought, this time in blue, for the American cause. When he died in 1906, Wheeler, aged nearly seventy, was buried at Arlington National Cemetery, one of the few ex-Confederates to earn this honor. Pond Spring, the Wheeler home in North Alabama, is now a museum.

Clement C. Clay returned to North Alabama but never recovered financially, emotionally or physically. He lived at his home, Wildwood, located near Gurley, Alabama, and died there on January 3, 1882, shortly after his sixty-fifth birthday. He is buried at Huntsville's Maple Hill Cemetery. His wife, Virginia, remarried and wrote a book, *A Belle of the Fifties*, about their lives together.

Jefferson Davis was released from prison while his trial for treason was postponed time and time again. Charges against him were finally dropped. He spent much time in Europe, went to work briefly for an insurance company that eventually failed and died in New Orleans at age eighty-one on December 6, 1889. He was buried in New Orleans and eventually reinterred at Hollywood Cemetery in Richmond, Virginia. On October 17, 1978, a joint resolution signed by Congress and President Jimmy Carter restored Davis's U.S. citizenship, retroactive to December 25, 1868. The Davis home and museum, Beauvoir, was extensively damaged by Hurricane Katrina in 2005. Located between Biloxi and Gulfport, the home of his later years will hopefully be restored. Many of the museum articles were scattered and irreparably destroyed.

Thunderbolt of the Confederacy

U sing dull knives smuggled out of the mess hall, six prisoners housed in the Ohio State Penitentiary began to dig under their bunks. Among those men were Thomas Hines, Dick Morgan and John Hunt Morgan, known by his nickname the "Thunderbolt of the Confederacy." It took patience and diligence to dig through the concrete floor, but they were persistent. On a cold November night in 1863, the prisoners of war were finally ready to make their escape. The story could have ended there, but General John Morgan would not leave well enough alone.

John Hunt Morgan was born in Huntsville, Alabama, on June 1, 1825. Several days after his birth, the Morgan family moved into their home at 558 Franklin Street, located in the heart of present-day Twickenham Historic District. He was the oldest of ten children born to Calvin Morgan and Henrietta Hunt Morgan. But their time in Huntsville would not last long. The family lost their home in 1831 when Calvin Morgan's business fell on hard times.

At that time, the Morgans left the Tennessee Valley and moved to Lexington, Kentucky, home to Henrietta Hunt Morgan's family. Young John Morgan's propensity for fighting made itself known early, for in 1844 he was suspended from Transylvania College for dueling with another student.

Like many of the men who would later serve in the War Between the States, Morgan enlisted in the army to fight in the Mexican-American War. He participated in the Battle of Buena Vista, also known as the Battle of

Angostura. In that February 23, 1847 battle, five thousand Americans serving under Major General Zachary Taylor fought, and sent running, twelve thousand Mexican soldiers under the command of self-proclaimed president of Mexico Santa Anna. Taylor's men were supported by the Mississippi Rifles, led by Colonel Jefferson Davis, a man who would play a major part in an upcoming war that would change the course of America's history. Major Braxton Bragg, another name that would become synonymous with the future American Civil War, was ordered by General Taylor to "double shot your guns and give them hell!" The famous quote would be rewritten slightly and serve as Taylor's campaign slogan, propelling him to the White House as president of the United States in 1848.

Although the Americans stubbornly held their position and gave the Mexicans the hell Taylor had prescribed, Santa Anna boasted that the battle was a Mexican victory and took his army with him in retreat to Agua Nueva.

At the conclusion of the war, John Hunt Morgan returned to Kentucky and, in 1848, married Rebecca Bruce. Tragedy struck five years after their marriage. Rebecca Morgan gave birth to a stillborn son, and an infection in her leg necessitated its amputation. Becky did not die, but her health problems would eventually take their toll. She died on July 21, 1861.

There was apparently no closeness between Morgan and his wife's family. Becky's health problems had put a strain on relations, and perhaps his in-laws also disapproved of his continued interest in military matters. He raised a company of infantry, the Lexington Rifles, and spent much of his time in drill. In 1861 the Civil War was already in progress, and with Becky's death, Morgan had no more ties to his wife and her need for constant care. As colonel of the newly established Second Kentucky Cavalry Regiment, Morgan began to implement the guerilla tactics he knew best.

On December 7, 1862, Morgan led his men at the Battle of Hartsville, Tennessee. Snow covered the ground as his force of fourteen hundred men marched toward the camp of Union colonel Absolom B. Moore, 104th Regiment, Illinois Infantry, located near the Cumberland River. Greatly outnumbered and miserably cold, Morgan's shivering men and their horses crossed the icy Cumberland River at 3:00 a.m. along with the men under the leadership of Basil Duke. Some Confederates did not cross, waiting to capture any Union soldiers who might try to escape to Lebanon, while others waited near Hartsville on the Gallatin Road for the same reason.

The battle began at about 6:45 a.m. "The Rebels are coming!" a servant shouted to the Union soldiers eating breakfast. An order was issued to sound the long drumroll—the prelude to battle. Four hundred yards from the camp, the Confederate cavalry was forming a line as the bugle sounded double-quick and then full speed. The Union soldiers waited as the Confederates advanced another three hundred yards. At the sound of the dreaded Rebel yell, the Confederate attack began.

The Battle of Hartsville lasted one hour, fifteen minutes. At the conclusion, a Confederate soldier said, "Never in my life have I looked upon anything so beautiful, so charming and so soul-satisfying as that white rag given to the breeze by the hand of a surrendered Yankee."

Morgan and his men captured eighteen hundred men, along with their arms and ammunition. Morgan's men had suffered because of their inadequate clothing, now frozen after the river crossing. His order to the Union prisoners of war was succinct: "Come out of those overcoats!"

Among the captives was Union colonel Absalom Moore, who was sent to a prison where he remained until his exchange early the following year. Moore made his belated report on February 25, 1863, and explained his defeat by writing that he was badly outnumbered. He reported that he was attacked by a Confederate army of five to six thousand strong, a far cry from the actual fourteen hundred. President Lincoln allowed him the opportunity to resign.

The Rebel victory was a much-needed boost to the sagging morale of the Southland. For this, Confederate president Jefferson Davis would personally reward John Hunt Morgan with the rank of brigadier general.

In the same month, Morgan married Tennessean Martha "Mattie" Ready, the daughter of U.S. representative Charles Ready. The wedding ceremony was a true celebration. Confederate general Leonidas Polk, known as the "Fighting Bishop," performed the ceremony. In attendance were Confederate president Jefferson Davis, General Braxton Bragg, General John Breckinridge, General William Hardee and General Benjamin "Frank" Cheatham.

Morgan and his men had already made a name for themselves. They were handpicked and carefully trained by their leader. George "Lightning" Ellsworth, a member of Morgan's Raiders, was an accomplished telegrapher who intercepted important information and, in turn, sent out misinformation to the Union army. The raiders blew up the Big South Tunnel near Gallatin, Tennessee, and otherwise wreaked havoc on the Union-held railroad lines. According to some sources, like Robin Hood before them, Morgan and his men stole supplies from the Union army and distributed them to the hungry citizens in the towns through which they passed.

John Hunt Morgan, the Thunderbolt of the Confederacy. *Library of Congress.*

Most of his notoriety would be gained by his actions in the summer of 1863, known as the Great Raid of 1863. Morgan and his raiders crossed the Ohio River and rode through southern Indiana and Ohio, making him the first and only Confederate to penetrate so far into the Union territory. In those three weeks, the raiders took approximately twelve hundred prisoners of war and raided seventeen towns. About seven hundred of his men were captured on July 19, but Morgan held out until July 26, when he and several of his men surrendered near Salineville, Ohio. It was at this time that they became guests of the State of Ohio.

On November 27, Morgan and his men were ready to make their escape from their cells in the Ohio State Penitentiary in Columbus. After several days of digging through concrete, lime mortar and brick, they reached the foundation of the building. This had to be dug through before they could begin their horizontal dig and final upward tunnel to the surface. After several weeks, the tunnel was finished. John Morgan, who was housed on the second floor, switched places with his brother, Dick, when it was time to be confined to their cells for the night. Dick would not be part of the escape party. Sometime after midnight, John Morgan arranged his bunk to appear as though he were sleeping soundly. He slipped into the tunnel under Dick's bunk and made his way down until he met the other five men in the tunnel.

From the surface, they still had to cross a high wall, but on the other side an unexpected surprise waited for them: Union guards warmed themselves next to a bonfire.

Their very lives depended on their sure-footed silence. They scattered, moving away from their prison home. Thomas Hines and John Morgan bought train tickets to Cincinnati and sat down beside a Union soldier. As they passed the Ohio State Penitentiary, the officer, who had no idea who his new friends were, glibly pointed out that the Confederate raider John Hunt Morgan was a prisoner there. Morgan's quick-witted reply was essentially, "May they guard him always as they do right now."

On September 4, 1864, Morgan's luck ran out. He and his men were in Greeneville, Tennessee, for a brief rest. Morgan and some of his men were staying at the mansion of a local widow when the Union army surrounded the house sometime in the night. Some stories indicate that the Union soldiers had been tipped off by a Union sympathizer—none other than their hostess, who received a handsome reward. Morgan and several others hurried quietly out the back door and ran to a nearby chapel, where they hid in the basement. Morgan heard the footsteps of the soldiers overhead looking for him. He knew it wouldn't be long before they found him. Although one of his men tried to talk him out of it, Morgan decided to slip in among the Union soldiers and try to blend in until he could get away. Unfortunately, someone recognized him, and he was shot to death on the spot.

Morgan's body was thrown onto the back of a horse and paraded up and down the streets as the Union detachment celebrated its kill. He was stripped and thrown into a ditch. Confederate Major Withers, one of the only staff officers taken prisoner, asked that he be allowed to return his commander's body to Morgan's widow, who was at that time in Abingdon, Virginia.

A memorial service was held in Abingdon for the slain general before he was transported to Richmond for a military funeral. Finally, in 1868, Morgan's brother brought him back to Lexington, Kentucky, for his final interment. Morgan was admired by the South, considered reckless by his superiors and dreaded by his enemies. But everyone knew who he was. At his third and final funeral, four years after he was killed, over two thousand people turned out to bid farewell to Huntsville's own Thunderbolt of the Confederacy.

Revenge at Horseshoe Bend

News of the August 30 massacre of nearly five hundred settlers, soldiers and slaves at Fort Mims by Creek Indians, also known as Red Sticks, spread rapidly throughout the Mississippi Territory in the late summer of 1813. It was the ultimate fear of every settler—to be killed, or worse, captured and tortured until death granted mercy. The names of the dead were reported, and some shook their heads in recognition. Descriptions of the grisly murders did not need to be exaggerated; they were too horrible without it. All over the territory, which would soon become the states of Mississippi and Alabama, residents warily made preparations for battle, just in case.

On October 7, less than two months after the Fort Mims massacre, the dreaded news that the Creek Indians were on the warpath again came to the residents of Huntsville. Word spread that the Creeks were within a day's ride of the town. Instantly, panic spread throughout the community. Kettles were left to boil over open fires in the kitchens as women grabbed their children to run toward Nashville. Mules were left in the fields, still hitched to the plows, and horses were hastily saddled, if at all, for a quick escape. In their panic, some grabbed other people's children and left their own, hoping that a good Samaritan would save them.

Soon the road was crowded with people running for their lives, anxious to put as much distance as possible between them and the hostile Creeks. The image of being scalped, mutilated and tortured was burned into their minds, and they called to everyone along the way to hurry and join them to seek safety in Tennessee.

The cause for this panic turned out to be a hoax. History does not record who brought the cruel rumor to Huntsville, but although the alleged attack was not real, the threat surely was. Something had to be done to quell the violent Indians.

General Andrew Jackson was recovering from a wound he had received in a duel when he heard the news about Fort Mims and the scare at Huntsville. Although his shoulder had been shattered and he was undoubtedly in great pain, he immediately went to work on plans to gather his militia for a journey into the Creek Indian lands.

From his home near Winchester, Tennessee, David Crockett heard the news of Fort Mims and gathered his guns and ammunition. His wife, Polly, begged him not to leave his family, but he reminded her that if something weren't done immediately, the Indians would eventually kill his own family in their home. He refused to wait for his wife to give him consent. Crockett went to Winchester to answer the call to muster.

Jackson and his men marched thirty-two miles in nine hours to arrive on October 11 in Huntsville, where they encamped at the present-day intersection of Holmes Avenue and Lincoln Street. Among the local men who put their lives on hold to join General Jackson was Dr. Thomas Fearn, who served as a battalion surgeon and personally tended General Jackson as he continued his recovery from the earlier duel. Dr. Fearn had studied medicine in Philadelphia and had only been in Huntsville about two years when he joined Jackson's men. Dr. Henry Chambers served as a surgeon on General Jackson's staff and had an ambitious political future ahead for him. Major Neal Rose, a Scotsman who later became owner of the Planters' Hotel, served in the quartermaster's department.

Major Gibson and his men were camped at Beatty's Spring (present-day Brahan Spring in Huntsville). He asked for two scouts to travel with him across the Tennessee River to spy on the Indians and their movements. Crockett volunteered his skills as a woodsman and rifleman. The next morning, they crossed Ditto Landing and, later that night, met up with an Indian trader who would be their guide. Early the following morning, the thirteen men were divided into two groups, and they agreed to meet fifteen miles beyond with information they had gleaned. The two groups moved cautiously through the Creeks' hunting grounds, staying away from known roads. Later that night, the men met up again. Having learned nothing of value, the men decided to press on. Crockett arrived at the home of a white man who was married to a Creek woman. Ten Creek warriors had left the house less than one hour before Crockett's arrival.

Crockett and his team pressed on and came upon two slaves who had been captured by the Creeks. One was sent back to Ditto Landing to give his story to Jackson and his men, while the other went with Crockett back to the camp of friendly Creek Indians. The slave, who was fluent in the Creek language, was able to find out that they were expecting a large war party at any moment. The plan of the Creek Indians was to annihilate General Jackson and his army.

Immediately, Crockett and his scouts saddled their horses and ran at full gallop back to warn the militia. Within a day, they reached the camp of Colonel John Coffee, who listened—unimpressed. Crockett was angry that Coffee didn't regard his news as important. He was angrier still when Major Gibson returned the next day with the same information. This time, Coffee listened and believed the news.

The Creek Indians were engaged and defeated at Tallushatchee on November 3 by Colonel John Coffee's men and, on November 11, at Hillabee by General White's men.

In the frenzy of the battle, an orphaned baby was discovered by one of Jackson's men. The surviving Creek women refused to take the baby, who cried from hunger and need of comfort. The baby was kept alive with a gruel made of brown sugar, water and crumbled biscuits. Though Andrew Jackson could be tough as nails when he needed to be, he also had a tender side, and so it was then that he decided to adopt the baby named Lincoya and raise the son of his enemy as his own.

Jackson wrote to his wife, Rachel, in December to prepare her for the new addition to the family:

> *He is the only branch of his family left, and the others, when offered to them to take care of, would have nothing to do with him, but wanted him to be killed…Quals, my interpreter, carried him on his back and brought him to me. Charity and Christianity says he ought to be taken care of and I send him to my little Andrew and I hope will adopt him as one of our family.*

Lincoya was sent to Huntsville to live at the LeRoy Pope household until arrangements could be made to get him to Nashville.

On November 13, an incident occurred that is retold to schoolchildren to this day. Captain Samuel Dale, a tall Virginian who spent much of his life trading with the Creeks, along with about seventy of his men, set out to drive the hostile Indians out of the region of the lower Alabama River so that settlers could gather their crops in safety. Most of his men had been sent across the river to the western bank in two canoes. Captain Dale and eleven of his men were still on the eastern bank when they heard the warning that Indians were approaching. A large canoe, carrying eleven Indians, floated downstream. Two of the Indians jumped out of the canoe and began to swim to shore. One was shot, the other escaped. The remaining nine Indians lay flat on the bottom of the canoe to avoid gunfire, and the white men assumed they were wounded or dead. Captain Dale ordered the men from the opposite side to get into the large canoe and approach the Indians. The white men turned and went back to shore when they discovered the Indians were alive. Dale was incensed at his own men and jumped into the smaller canoe on his side of the river to attack the Indians himself.

Captain Dale, along with James Smith, nineteen-year-old Jeremiah Austill and a black man named Caesar, who operated the canoe ferry, quickly reached the nine Indians in the large canoe. One of the Indians recognized Dale and shouted, "Now for it, big Sam!"

Caesar held the two canoes together while the hand-to-hand combat commenced. The priming, used to ignite the gunpowder, was wet, rendering the weapons useless, except for the bayonets. Those who had no bayonets used the stock end as clubs. The ensuing battle was fierce. The Indians cheered their own from one side of the river as Dale's men cheered from the other side.

When the fighting ended, the bodies of the nine Indians were tossed into the river. The four men in the smaller canoe escaped with minor injuries.

The Creek Indian Wars continued. On November 29, the Indians were defeated at Attassee by General Floyd's men, at Talladega by General Jackson's men and, on December 23, at Eccanachaca by General Claiborne's men. The Indians had been told by their prophets that the earth would swallow the white men who dared to enter the Holy Ground, and so their confidence began to crumble when this was proven false.

The army began again in January 1814 with a defeat at Emuckfau by Jackson's men on January 18 and again on the twenty-fourth at Enotochopco. Jackson's army had been fortified by the addition of friendly Creek and Cherokee warriors, and certainly, had it not been for them, Jackson's army would have been defeated.

The winter had been difficult for Jackson and his men. Jackson suffered from malaria, dysentery and pulmonary hemorrhaging. At six feet, one inch tall, his weight would sometimes plummet to 120 pounds. Still, he thought of his suffering men and sometimes gave his horse to a sick man while he walked through the mud for miles. He even gave his own food to the sick.

At one particularly low point, some of the men threatened to leave. One man, determined to make General Jackson personally aware of their misery, found Old Hickory seated on a log eating acorns. General Jackson listened patiently to the man's complaints, then reached into his pocket and offered him the only food the general himself had, more acorns. It made a lasting impact on the young soldier, who went back to the others and reported that the general himself was suffering as much as they were.

Because the initial sixty-day enlistment was now expired by over one month, some of the men, including David Crockett, left the camp and headed home. While some did not return, Crockett gathered more provisions, newer clothing and more horses and headed back to General Jackson's camp.

In March, the Creeks established their camp in the bend of the Tallapoosa River (near present-day Alexander City) known as Horseshoe Bend. Log and brush fortifications were built, but the prophets continually reminded the Creeks that the white man could not conquer them. The encampment was surrounded on three sides by water, with no way out. Approximately one thousand Creeks set to work constructing an earthworks system for protection during an assault. But General Jackson was "determined to exterminate them." When he saw the physical layout of their camp, he remarked, "They have penned themselves up for slaughter."

Jackson sent John Coffee and his men on the early morning of March 27 to surround the Indians on the far sides of the Tallapoosa River to prevent their escape by water. Spies in Coffee's assemblage crossed the river and destroyed the Creeks' canoes. They set fires on the outside edges of the encampment to signal the beginning of the bloody, final battle.

The regular army, under the direction of Colonel Williams and Major Montgomery, began the assault. Twenty-eight-year-old Major Montgomery led the charge and was the first man to climb the breastworks of the Creek stronghold. As he raised his sword to rally his men to follow, a bullet through his head killed him instantly. Jackson's Guard, the Tennessee Militia, charged into the horseshoe itself, while Coffee's men charged from the river. The men of Jackson's Guard, wearing top hats as part of their official uniforms, had the only artillery.

The Creeks placed the captured slaves from Fort Mims in the front lines to receive the first gunfire. They had hoped that the white soldiers would spare the slaves while the Indians stalled for more time. But with the memory of Fort Mims still fresh in their minds, the militia did not stop until every Creek warrior—reported to be over one thousand—was dead. Jackson had lost thirty-two men, while the friendly Creeks lost five and the Cherokees were down by eighteen. Witnesses said that the river's water ran red with the blood of the slain men. Before long, the battle—and the Creek Indian Wars—was finally over.

A young army officer named Sam Houston had been wounded by an arrow to his leg as one of the first soldiers to reach the log fortifications constructed by the Creeks. He remarked that when the sun set that evening, "it set over the ruin of the Creek Nation."

William Weatherford, also known as Red Eagle and chief of the Creek Indians, was ordered to be brought to General Jackson as a prisoner. He arrived at Jackson's tent willingly. Jackson was surprised at his audacity and informed Weatherford that he deserved death for the inhumane conduct at Fort Mims. Weatherford surprised Jackson when he replied, "I am in your power, do with me as you please. I am a soldier. I have done the whites all the harm I could. I have fought them and fought them bravely. If I had an army I would yet fight. I would contend to the last. My people are all gone. I can only weep over the misfortunes of my nation.

General Jackson answered, "You are at liberty to depart unmolested. You may place yourself at the head of your war party again and fight us as hard as you please, but if you fall into our hands, you will receive no mercy. The only safety for you and your people is in unconditional submission."

The Creek chief acknowledged that there was no other choice for the Creeks and agreed to surrender according to the conditions laid out by General Jackson. He asked that Jackson give food to the starving Creek women and children who were hiding in the woods, and Jackson agreed without hesitation.

In early May, General Jackson and his men arrived, as a triumphant army, in Huntsville. A grand celebration was held in their honor at the home of LeRoy Pope, and toasts were made to the heroes of Horseshoe Bend.

Lincoya was raised in privilege at the Hermitage, though at times he had tendencies to revert to the habits of his Native American ancestors. He was known to chase the chickens with a bow and arrow while wearing a headdress made of turkey feathers. Jackson had hoped to have him enrolled at West Point Military Academy, but according to some sources, his Indian heritage caused him to be denied admission.

When Lincoya was fourteen, Jackson took him to Nashville to pursue a trade. Lincoya decided to work as an apprentice saddle maker, and he rode his horse home to the Hermitage on weekends. Sadly, he became ill and died, possibly from pneumonia, at the age of sixteen.

Revenge at Horseshoe Bend

Major Lemuel Montgomery, who died at the first charge of Horseshoe Bend, was honored when Montgomery County was named for him. Ironically, the city of Montgomery was named for his ancestor, who died in the struggle for American independence.

One year after the war started, the remaining Creek Indians signed the Treaty of Fort Jackson. General Andrew Jackson would go on to become president of the United States and would order the controversial forced removal of Indians along what became known as the Trail of Tears. In 2006, Jackson's home, the Hermitage, was designated as a historic site relating to the Trail of Tears. David Crockett and Sam Houston entered politics and left Tennessee to seek their fortunes in the republic of Texas.

The Mysterious Disappearance of Granville Garth

On October 13, 1855, the first train arrived at Huntsville's Eastern Division headquarters of the Memphis & Charleston Railroad. Folks lined the streets to celebrate and watch as the General Garth chugged triumphantly into town. A spectator was quoted as saying that it was "the greatest day in the history of Huntsville since John Hunt!" The train was named for William Willis Garth, who served in the Confederate army as a colonel on Longstreet's staff. After the Civil War, he became an Alabama politician and Huntsville attorney. Members of his extended family lived at the fabulous Monte Sano Hotel and led the local social scene for many decades. But one member of the Garth family who did not live in Huntsville made more headlines than all others combined when he mysteriously disappeared one cold, dark Christmas night, never to be heard from again.

Granville Garth was born in Memphis, Tennessee, on August 11, 1863, to Kentucky natives Horace and Alice Jones Garth. His sister, Lena, was three when the family welcomed their only son, and when Granville was sixteen, the family moved to New York. Granville was a member of the graduating class of 1886 at Columbia University, where he excelled in baseball and academics.

Founded originally in New York as King's College in 1754 under a royal charter granted by King George II of England, Columbia University was affiliated with the Anglican Church. Among the more famous graduates were Alexander Hamilton, first secretary of the treasury, and several men who drafted the Declaration of Independence. After America's war with England, the name was changed to Columbia.

After his graduation, Granville went to work on Wall Street and found his place at the Mechanics National Bank of New York, where his father, Horace, served as bank president. On April 26, 1893, Granville married Lilly McComb at her parents' home at 180 West Fifty-ninth Street in New York. The *New York Times* wrote the following day that it was a small wedding, featuring a ten-foot arbor of white roses and a bank of roses on the fireplace mantel in the drawing room, where the ceremony took place. Among those in attendance were Granville's college friends, members of the '86 Bachelor Club.

Though visits were few and far between, Granville occasionally spent time with his sister, whose last name remained the same after she married a distant cousin, William Willis Garth Jr., and made her home at the Piedmont Estate on Whitesburg Drive in Huntsville. Lena, a graduate of Vassar College, was described as a stately blonde and a perfect hostess. She was active in the Twickenham Town Chapter, Daughters of the American Revolution, and founded several local garden clubs. She was known for her command of the English language and proper grammar, and she was demanding of her servants and children when it came to etiquette, always setting a good example herself.

Lena employed a maid named Rosetta, who had worked in the cotton fields before Lena hired her to work inside her Piedmont home. One night, Lena and her husband were entertaining dinner guests, and soon after Rosetta served the salad, Lena informed her that she had forgotten to bring the salad oil. After a conspicuous fifteen-minute absence, Rosetta reappeared with a rusty coal oilcan, which she had retrieved from the cellar and carried into the dining room on a silver platter. Fortunately, Lena also possessed graciousness and a good sense of humor.

Lena's husband was a Civil War veteran, a graduate of Sewanee College in Tennessee and owned a trotting horse farm. His horses won many races, though, ironically, William never bet on any races himself.

But while wealth eases some of life's transitions and passages, it doesn't necessarily buy health and long-lasting happiness. Horace Garth, father of Lena and Granville, suffered a stroke that partially paralyzed him. He was no longer able to fulfill his duties as president of the Mechanics National Bank of New York, and with the approval of the bank's board, his son Granville succeeded him as the president. It seemed like a sound decision. After all, since graduating from college, Granville continued to prosper in the business world, and with a little help from his father, his tenure on Wall Street had blossomed. In 1903, he took over the reins as president of the oldest bank in

The Mysterious Disappearance of Granville Garth

New York (founded in 1810), serving as the youngest president in the bank's history. By now, he and Lilly were the parents of two young daughters, and at age forty, his future looked solid and bright.

Within a few months, however, cracks appeared in Granville Garth's persona. Perhaps it was the stress of his demanding job or, if rumors were correct, the result of a crumbling marriage. Whatever the cause, it seemed that he was on the verge of, if not in the throes of, a nervous breakdown. On December 14, 1903, the directors of the bank, which included his father, met and wrote a proclamation encouraging Granville to take a leave of absence for at least four months to rest. Dr. Francis Delafield prescribed rest and a voyage at sea.

Granville Garth agreed to take the sage advice of the doctor and his business associates and left New York on December 19, without his family by his side, to make his way by sea to Galveston, Texas. Perhaps he was unaware that at the beginning of his voyage, a man named Thomas Lawson, a confidential representative for Blair and Company of New York, was assigned to watch him closely. Lawson had known Garth's family well, though he did not know Granville.

The following details were taken from several articles that appeared in the *New York Times* within days of the launching of the *Denver*. Captain Evans was concerned about Granville Garth from the moment he boarded the ship. His behavior was strange, and Evans was unsure about taking him on as a passenger. Garth's friends, who went with him to give him a hearty send-off, assured the captain that he and his crew would not have to look after Garth; he was in good hands with Thomas Lawson, and his trip south was for a few weeks of rest. Garth himself told the captain that he was ill, so he apparently knew he needed help.

Soon after the voyage began, Thomas Lawson's watchful eye was not accepted kindly or graciously by Granville Garth. Garth did not like Lawson and did not appreciate his continual presence everywhere he went. The passengers also noted Garth's "mental aberration," a polite term for mental illness, and he further drew attention to himself by tipping the waiters and crewmen outrageously, as much as several hundred dollars in the first few days. He rambled incoherently at times, called out for his invalid father and talked about being ruined. He would not eat food and only occasionally sipped tea. He paced the deck at all hours and in all kinds of weather. He was paranoid as well, and when he heard the sound of chains being dragged across the deck, Garth cried out, "My God, they are going to put me in irons!"

On Christmas morning, Garth appeared better. Perhaps it was the calming effect of the sea, the rolling waves or the fresh air that seemed to reach him. Maybe it was the spirit of Christmas that cheered him somewhat. The other passengers and crew of the *Denver* seemed relieved, but his improvement was short-lived.

Early that evening, Garth appeared restless, according to witnesses. The ship's purser was engaged in a conversation about him and was cautioned to keep an eye on him. Unbeknownst to them, Garth overheard this dialogue, and whatever was said upset him. At 8:30 p.m., he was seen on deck. One hour later, an alarm was given to crew members that Garth was missing.

While searchlights scanned the darkened waters for any sign of Granville Garth, others combed the entire ship hoping to find him safe and sound. No one had seen him jump or fall overboard. After three hours of careful, but frantic searching, the *Denver* continued on to cover the three hundred miles between it and the shore of Galveston, Texas.

Soon after the *Denver* docked at Galveston, reporters arrived to get the scoop. Granville Garth was missing, and everyone began to point fingers at everyone else. Lawson blamed the captain for his disappearance, and of course the captain blamed Lawson, saying that Lawson was the party responsible for Garth's behavior and safety. No doubt, neither one of them wanted the wrath of Granville's father upon them. Lawson refused to speak to reporters, but he did retrieve Garth's luggage.

Just after midnight, a telegram was sent to A.A. Knowles, the New York cashier of Mechanics National Bank. Other bank representatives were notified soon after, and the news was broken to Horace Garth as carefully as possible for fear that his precarious health would be worsened by this traumatic turn of events.

The bank's spin doctors got to work denying rumors of Garth's marital troubles and improprieties at the bank. He was wealthy in his own right, and the bank had never been on more solid grounds. His friends spoke to reporters about their concern for his health in recent weeks. Mentally, he seemed to be exhausted, unable to control his emotions, and his thoughts didn't seem to connect. His brother-in-law was quoted as saying, "The public does not yet know what his trouble was. He was a disappointed man and he played a game of chess and lost."

Whatever his personal troubles were, they were apparently well known in society and at the bank but were never reported in the papers, and those reasons are now lost to the past. Newspaper reports in Galveston, Texas, as well as in New York, speculated that he had either thrown himself overboard or had accidentally fallen off the ship. Whatever the cause, it was reported that he had drowned.

Within days, Granville's father announced a reward of $10,000 for anyone who could find his son's body or any piece of clothing containing certain papers. Granville's wife of nearly twelve years, along with daughters, Helen and Florence, remained in seclusion in their New York City apartment at 160 West Fifty-ninth Street. His mother's brother went to New Orleans to supervise search operations for his body. Advertisements were placed in newspapers, and search teams were sent out along the coastline. It was ultimately assumed that strong currents carried his body farther out into the ocean. No trace of Granville Garth was ever found.

Granville and Lilly Garth's daughters eventually moved to England and married. An enormous obelisk now stands tall in a cemetery in Memphis, Tennessee's Elmwood Cemetery. It announces that Granville was lost at sea on December 25, 1903.

In the meantime, Granville's sister, Huntsville resident Lena Garth, became the caregiver for her aging parents. In 1909, she purchased the empty Monte Sano Resort Hotel, the health resort named for the mountain it sat atop, for the sum of $20,000. The 233-room hotel became the new home for her parents. It was their hope that Horace Garth's health would improve, but it wasn't to be. Within two years after moving in, on July 31, 1911, he died at age seventy-two. He was buried in Memphis.

***

The Monte Sano Resort Hotel did not survive, in spite of its once glorious reputation. It was built eighteen hundred feet above sea level, and the nearby Cold Spring provided pure, fresh water to the guests who began arriving on June 1, 1887, for the grand opening. Several grand balls were held that first season. When over four hundred guests arrived in early July to dance, canvas was laid out to protect the Brussels carpets. Many partygoers danced out on the porches for lack of floor space inside the ballroom. Over three hundred soldiers were stationed on the mountain due to a yellow fever epidemic at Fort Barancas in Florida, adding significantly to the festivities and excitement that year.

Monte Sano Resort Hotel. *Photo courtesy Huntsville–Madison County Public Library.*

No expense was spared to entertain and pamper the wealthy who came to visit. The first season, which ended in October, was so successful that a two-story house was built, which contained thirty-six rooms to accommodate the overflow from the resort. It was named Memphis Row in honor of the city that provided the most guests.

The biggest problem, however, was transportation up and down the mountain. A carriage pulled by six horses, known as a tallyho, was used the first year, but it was too expensive and, all around, unsatisfactory. Ruins of the old trains on the mountain indicate that it was quite rocky and therefore a most uncomfortable ride. By August 7 of the next year, a railroad had been completed to the top. A train wreck occurred soon after the service started. Although no one was seriously injured, it caused many people to avoid the trip and, unfortunately, a visit to the Monte Sano Resort Hotel. By 1896, the steel rails had been pulled up.

The hotel suffered terribly from poor decisions made at the top. Although the resort boasted many famous guests from around the world, it did not open one year at all because of quarreling among the stockholders. In 1898, electricity was brought to the mountain resort, but sadly, the 1899 season would be the last for the Monte Sano Resort Hotel.

The hotel remained furnished but vacant for another ten years, until Horace and Alice Garth came to Huntsville. Mr. Garth died in the summer of 1911.

On May 28, 1917, a surprising story appeared in the *Huntsville Mercury*. A plan to reopen the hotel was announced if $25,000 could be raised for improvements. In the next few months, advertisements were published inviting guests to the resort, and there was even a story about the new style of dress adopted by visitors. The resurrection of the great hotel was apparently short-lived.

For the next twenty-seven years, the vacant mansion saw no visitor but the occasional winter fog that rolled in. A caretaker stayed near the mansion to watch over it as it sat, fully furnished, decaying in total abandonment. In 1944, the executors of the Garth estate sold the once beautiful old hotel for only $9,000. It was torn down and sold for scrap.

The old railroad bed, now a rocky footpath for nature lovers, still snakes its way to the top of Monte San Mountain. Although one can imagine the scenic beauty enjoyed by the visitors as they made the train trip, the remnants of harrowing hairpin turns indicate the danger as well.

Today, the only evidence that remains of the gathering place of some of the most famous people of that time is a lone three-story chimney, lovingly tended and preserved.

The Ghosts on the Hill

For many years, Colonel LeRoy Pope has been known as the father of Huntsville. Local children learn it in school, and Pope's image is at the center of a magnificent two-story mosaic in the Madison County Courthouse. In the last few years, however, historians have chipped away at the brittle veneer of deception to find that facts don't support the glorious myth.

The mansion built by LeRoy Pope in Huntsville sits high atop Echols Hill. When it was completed in 1814, he boasted that from his porch, he had the finest view of all of Huntsville. One of his enemies was about to change all that. When Joshua Cox built his home below the bluff, he made sure that the ceilings were extra tall. The two-story home below blocked Pope's view of downtown Huntsville and has been forevermore known as the Spite House. But Joshua Cox wouldn't have the last word. Apparently, Mr. Cox did not have clear title to the property; the man who did was none other than LeRoy Pope. In a firestorm of anger and bitterness, Mr. Cox was evicted from his beautiful home, and the Spite House became the new home of Pope's daughter.

LeRoy Pope was born in Northumberland County, Virginia. He moved with his family to Amherst County, Virginia, and served as an aid to General George Washington during the American Revolution. He was present at the Battle of Yorktown. After the war, many Virginians moved to Elbert County, Georgia, to try their hands at growing tobacco in the vast open fields. Dionysius Oliver had founded the town of Petersburg in 1786, named

LeRoy Pope. *Photo courtesy Huntsville–Madison County Public Library.*

Home of LeRoy Pope. *HABS-HAER photograph.*

for a town in Virginia. Pope, along with his friends and relatives, were there by 1790.

Petersburg soon became the third largest city in Georgia, after Savannah and Augusta. Located at the fork of the Broad and Savannah Rivers, it became a bustling little community with a number of stores and beautiful homes. After a few years, though, the soil was depleted, and the rich topsoil, overplanted and fragile, blew away. The farmers looked to the west for more land and the chance to grow rich on cotton.

In 1805, pioneer John Hunt wandered into the woods surrounding the cool, clear water known as the Big Spring in the Mississippi Territory. He built his cabin, cleared some land for a garden and named the stake Hunt's Spring. It was still Indian-owned property, but after it was ceded to the U.S. government, Hunt knew it would be his to buy when the time came. Soon, other settlers poured in to make ready for their chance to buy land too. Among them was a large group of people from Petersburg, Georgia—transplants from Virginia—who would dominate the political scene for decades to come. One of the richest and most powerful of these transplants was LeRoy Pope.

Details differ on how John Hunt lost his cabin and land at the Big Spring in present-day Madison County, Alabama. The outcome, however, was the same. LeRoy Pope went to the land sale in Nashville and came back as the new owner of John Hunt's property. John Hunt was evicted and lived the remainder of his life in Tennessee. Pope owned a huge chunk of the most desirable real estate that would soon become the town and lobbied to have the county seat located there. That was all well and good, but then he had the name changed to Twickenham, the name of an estate outside of London that belonged to the famous poet Alexander Pope.

By now perhaps, local folks saw the clear picture of his character—warts and all. They didn't like what they saw, or perhaps they didn't appreciate the power that he wielded. Anne Royall, an early writer who visited the area, wrote a letter to a friend telling about her experience at a missionary meeting where money was collected by the people in attendance. A hat was passed, and folks dropped in what they had. LeRoy Pope popped a quarter into the hat. The following day, the women of town hissed about LeRoy Pope's contribution. "'Such a man—a man of his wealth—to give a quarter—Did you ever see the like! They would have given all they had!' It was, beyond a doubt, the worst laid out quarter he ever spent," Royall wrote.

The people of Twickenham began to resist Colonel Pope's control over them. They demanded that the town's name be changed, and they settled on Huntsville to honor John Hunt. Some saw LeRoy Pope's interests in the bank, the layout of the town, the Indian Creek Canal and other issues of a struggling new community as the actions of a responsible citizen. Others saw it as interference. Even his own son-in-law, John Williams Walker, was wary of him. Pope had once sued Walker's father in Georgia, and Walker wrote to a friend that he loved the daughter but not the man, and he refused to bow down to him.

In comparison, Pope's wife, Judith Sales Pope, was his exact opposite. She seemed to be more grounded, in spite of the fact that she lived in what was known as the grandest home in all of Alabama. When she died, her obituary reported that she was unaffected by her wealth (quite a compliment apparently) and seemingly unaware of her status.

According to one source, LeRoy Pope objected when it was time to pay veterans of the American Revolution for their service. Even though they had been promised bounty warrants at the time they signed up to fight (only if America won the Revolution), the government didn't make good on that promise until some decades after the war ended. Pope's feeling was that they should have been expected to fight for their country and not demand payment in return, but he was overruled. Perhaps he was afraid that the truth would come out.

Many years after Pope's death in 1844, the Twickenham Town Chapter, Daughters of the American Revolution, decided to mark Pope's grave at Maple Hill Cemetery. Enough time had passed, his reputation had been forgotten and anyone who was an aide to the esteemed father of our country deserved to be recognized with a plaque. But when the *i*'s were dotted and the *t*'s were crossed, a discovery was made, and the whole matter was promptly dropped. There was no record of Pope's service in the American Revolution.

The estate built by LeRoy Pope remains a Huntsville landmark today, as does the infamous Spite House. Nearly two hundred years after it was completed, the mansion remains isolated on the hill, surrounded by tall trees that keep the ground below dark and cool.

For most people, the story of these early settlers is securely hidden—or perhaps forgotten. Those who communicate with ghosts and have taken the time to listen tell the truth from a different, more ethereal standpoint. The ghosts of slaves quietly, deliberately and slowly walk the grounds of the Pope mansion. They know they are dead but wait for Jesus to return for them.

Others have seen the slaves walk slowly down in the direction of the bluff, only to disappear. Another visitor has seen a black man in a suit walk the grounds and then disappear behind a tree. The most chilling warning of all comes from a disembodied specter that whispers to visitors to beware of LeRoy Pope. "He is a crook. He took everything but the water from the old man and if you're not careful, he'll steal you blind as well." LeRoy Pope has not lived up to his legend apparently, but who among us today will ever sort out the truth? Perhaps one day the ghost of LeRoy Pope himself will appear to give us his version of the truth. Until then, the legacy of the father of Huntsville will have to endure.

EPILOGUE

Pope's daughter, Mathilda, married John Williams Walker, a promising young politician who died prematurely of tuberculosis. One of their children, a namesake of his grandfather, was born in 1817. Leroy Pope Walker was appointed as the secretary of war of the Confederacy. As such, he ordered the first shot fired at Fort Sumter at 4:30 a.m. on the chilly morning of April 12, 1861. His speech that day revealed the sentiments of most Americans— that the conflict would be over in no time at all. "I will take my pocket handkerchief and wipe up all the blood shed as a result of the South leaving

Leroy Pope Walker. *Photo courtesy Huntsville–Madison County Public Library.*

the Union," he said. And then he promised that "the flag that flaunts the breeze today will fly over the dome of the old Capital by the first of May." Neither prediction would come true.

Seven bloody months later, Walker left his position. His resignation to Confederate president Jefferson Davis said, "In withdrawing from your Cabinet, I can, I feel assured, without any impeachment of my motives, say to you in writing what I have often said of you, that you were the only man I have ever met whose greatness grew upon me the nearer I approached him."

William Clarke Quantrill

Guerrilla Leader

The border wars in Missouri and Kansas were ruthless and every bit as bloody as major battles of the Civil War. To the residents of these states, devastation and death came without warning. Many notorious outlaws, such as Jesse and Frank James, came to prominence in the guerilla wars on the borders, but no name could strike as much fear as the name William Clarke Quantrill. When he was killed in the spring of 1865, residents in both the North and South breathed a sigh of relief. But it is quite possible that Quantrill was not killed that day by Union soldiers. In fact, evidence strongly suggests that he lived the remainder of his days in North Alabama.

William Quantrill was born in Canal Dover, Ohio, in 1837. Because his father was a schoolteacher, he benefited from a fairly good education himself. Unfortunately, after he moved to Kansas at the age of twenty, he began to support himself through a life of crime. He started off small—he stole cattle and then food to feed them. When the theft was discovered, he fled to Salt Lake City. A few months later, he was living in Lawrence, Kansas.

By this time, the country was embroiled in a bitter civil war. The state of Missouri was divided, neither Union nor Confederate. Although Missouri was not a slave state, not everyone agreed that the country shouldn't split. Sympathies swayed to the South when Union forces appropriated whatever they needed from residents, and then swayed again when the Confederates did the same. The result was a bitterly divided state. Because Kansas was a border state as well, hostilities oftentimes spilled over.

William Quantrill taught school in Lawrence, Kansas, for a short time but found more lucrative money in stealing slaves, mules and horses and then returning them to their owners for a reward. By now he had several partners. When his plot was uncovered by the law, he was banned from the state of Kansas. Quantrill and his followers left with the promise that they would return for revenge.

Quantrill made his headquarters in Missouri. Among his fellow outlaws were Jesse and Frank James, Dick Yeager, Cole Younger and Bill Anderson. They all had grievances to settle. Although they were not soldiers of the Confederate army, they harbored hatred of the Union soldiers and pro-Union citizens. Many were farm boys who had lost their homes and crops. They had been harassed, and some had lost family members. Among those who had lost loved ones were Bill Anderson and Cole Younger. Anderson's sisters and Younger's cousin were kept as prisoners in a run-down brick building in Kansas City. The building had collapsed, injuring or killing the women prisoners. They vowed to get even.

The people of Lawrence were aware of the threats made against them by Quantrill and his men. For some time, they were watchful; guards were ready to sound the alarm of Quantrill and his men's murderous approach, but as time went on without an attack, citizens of the town assumed that Quantrill's threats were idle words. Unfortunately for them, Quantrill and his men intended to make good on their threats. The date set for the attack was the early morning hours of August 21, 1863.

The methods of guerrilla warfare were treacherous and harsh. The attack on Lawrence, Kansas, was carefully planned. Spies were employed throughout the town, and at least one citizen supplied maps and valuable information. The townspeople would be dead before anyone had time to react.

Some reports put the number of Quantrill's men at three hundred, while other sources say there were as many as five hundred who rode toward the twelve hundred unsuspecting citizens of Lawrence, Kansas. Quantrill's unit carried the Union flag as a cover, but as it neared the town, the flag was lowered and a different, more ominous flag was raised in its place. It was a black flag with Quantrill's name stitched in red.

The raiders entered the town from the southeast and broke up into squads of four, six and eight. Then they scattered to the homes of sleeping citizens. The main body rode into the business section of town.

Senator James H. Lane, who had ordered his men to come down hard with brutality and force against secessionists, was one of Quantrill's specific targets. While the men searched his home, Lane escaped death by hiding behind a log in back of his house.

Judge Carpenter, a Union sympathizer who had ruled in favor of the Union cause in one of his court cases, was pulled from his bed. As he ran from the house and tried to escape, his wife ran to him and threw her arms around him. The guerrillas pulled her away roughly and shot him while she begged for mercy.

As the night of carnage continued, over 150 homes and businesses were torched by the marauders. The number of men and boys killed that terrible night was a staggering 185. As the men under Quantrill's command rode off, two-thirds of the town was left homeless. His name would never be forgotten.

The Civil War and its related border wars continued. Several raids by pro-Union men and soldiers were made in retaliation. Quantrill retreated to Texas. While in Texas, Confederate general E. Kirby Smith issued an order to allow Quantrill's men to help capture deserters and keep hostile Comanche Indians at arm's length. In the meantime, "Bloody Bill" Anderson, one of Quantrill's raiders, split from the group and formed his own band of raiders. There were now two groups of outlaws practicing guerrilla warfare on the citizens of Texas, and that was finally too much. Confederate forces were used to protect the Texans, and Quantrill was arrested. He escaped.

Quantrill and his men made it safely into Indian Territory and bid Texas goodbye. His followers, having lost confidence in him, elected George Todd as their new leader. Though he assembled a new group of raiders back in Missouri, their strength and numbers would never be the same. The war had continued for nearly three years by this time, and it appeared that even criminals were getting tired of the bloodshed. At some point, he rallied some followers to go with him to Washington to assassinate President Abraham Lincoln. The timeline for that event, as well as the circumstances of Quantrill's death, vary from one account to another.

As Quantrill passed through Kentucky in 1865 (accounts differ), he was ambushed and shot by Federal troops. He lingered for three weeks before he died, and at least one source says he left $500 in gold to his wife, who used the money to open a bordello in St. Louis. The news of his death was splashed in newspapers all across the country. Although there was no evidence that he had officially joined the Confederate army, he was considered pro-Southern in his sentiments. But the Confederate army didn't trust or approve of his methods either.

After his death and burial, his mother insisted on seeing his body. She was surprised to find that the corpse had red hair and a light complexion. Her son had coal-black hair.

Many people are convinced that Quantrill saw the opportunity to start over with a clean slate and took advantage of his second chance. According to Annie Guthrie, a resident of Guntersville, Alabama, the following story has been passed down through her family.

After the Civil War, a Confederate prisoner, who was among those paroled from the Elmira Prison Camp in New York, began his journey back to the South. Elmira, nicknamed "Hellmira" by those who survived, had a 25 percent death rate, slightly below the death rate of Andersonville, Georgia. The surgeon of Elmira boasted that he had killed more Confederates than any Union soldier. Clothing sent in by prisoners' families was burned unless it was gray in color, and consequently, many died of exposure. Deaths from scurvy, disease and malnutrition were excessive. Those who survived were lucky.

One of the Elmira alumni put a great deal of distance between himself and the infamous prison when he stopped in a community on North Alabama's Sand Mountain. He lived with a Methodist minister and his family. While there, he found grace in the eyes of God and became a Christian. In fact, he became a Methodist minister himself. The man went by the name of William Clark McCoy. He was educated, and in addition to being a Methodist minister, he also edited a newspaper. He fell in love with and married a fifteen-year-old girl who had suffered from polio as a child. Before long, they started a family.

It wasn't long, however, before rumors began to circulate about the similarities between the late William Clarke Quantrill and the Reverend William Clark McCoy. Both had black hair, and both men were missing a finger on one hand. Both men had a tattoo of an Indian maiden. When a newspaperman from Birmingham tried to interview Mrs. McCoy, the five-foot-tall woman chased him off with her cane.

There were other clues as well. In 1884, Frank James, a former member of Quantrill's Raiders, was held in a Huntsville jail to await trial on an accusation of robbing Alexander Smith, the government paymaster, near Muscle Shoals, Alabama, in 1881. While he was incarcerated, Reverend William Clark McCoy went to visit the prisoner. When he walked in, a surprised Frank James exclaimed, "Well Bill! I thought you were dead!"

Reverend McCoy/Quantrill quickly put his finger to his mouth in a gesture to signal silence. The two men talked quietly for about an hour, and then McCoy left the jail.

The most telling clue was McCoy's expertise with his ivory-handled pistols. He was standing in the church pulpit one day when Yankee carpetbaggers came in with the intention of inciting some trouble in the community. The Methodist minister warned them that it would be in their best interest to move on. To accentuate his point, he picked up an ear of corn. He scratched or somehow marked an X on one kernel and hung the ear of corn over the front door of the church. From the pulpit, he pulled his pistol and fired. The bullet found its mark on the kernel with an X. The carpetbaggers understood the implication and quickly left.

Reverend McCoy died in 1891 and was buried in Birmingham. His widow would neither confirm nor deny that her husband had been the legendary William Quantrill. Years later, her children spent a small fortune trying to learn his true identity. They even traveled to Missouri to interview the widow of Frank James. They would never know for sure.

Annie Guthrie, the granddaughter of the Reverend William Clark McCoy, would like to know the answer to that question too. Mrs. Guthrie still has the walking cane her grandmother used to chase the reporters away and once visited the horrible Elmira Prison where her grandfather was incarcerated.

Mrs. Guthrie's grandmother carried the secret of her husband's true identity with her to her grave. Upon her death, she was buried next to her beloved husband at Elmwood Cemetery in Birmingham. Although McCoy had originally been buried at another Birmingham cemetery, his widow had his body reinterred when the installation of a gate at the first cemetery required that his body be among those moved to another location.

After the death of William Clarke Quantrill, accounts of his crimes became almost legendary. He was blamed for more atrocities, killings and lootings than he could have possibly had time for. But those were not the only unanswered questions. Except for the raid on Lawrence, Kansas, today's Quantrill biographies rarely agree on many facts about him, including the spelling of his name. One fact, however, persists: the life and death of William Clarke Quantrill will forever remain one of history's enigmas.

George Steele and the Marble Palace

When renowned Huntsville architect George Steele died in October 1855, a simple slab was placed over his grave at Maple Hill Cemetery. Although he had managed the construction of many architectural masterpieces, he said that the buildings would be the most fitting and lasting memorials of his time on earth. While the physical relics of his talents are still appreciated today, it was the content of his unusual will that would draw more interest than his work for decades to come. Was his secret a shock to society in 1855? Perhaps not.

George Steele was born in Virginia in 1798. According to some sources, his mother died while he was young and his father remarried. Young George did not get along with his father's new wife, and so he set out in 1818 for the Alabama Territory, settling in Huntsville. George may have apprenticed as an architect, for modern historians cannot find any record of his having had any formal education. By 1824, he had built seven homes, including his first home on Randolph Street.

Unfortunately, George went to court nearly thirty-five times in an attempt to get the money owed to him by the people who bought his homes. Huntsville was in the throes of a financial panic, and times were rough for everyone. The price of cotton crashed, and those wealthy planters who had bought great tracts of land on the speculation that their cotton crops would provide revenue to pay off their debts lost everything.

George studied the Greek revival style of architecture. It was the rage all over the South, and he is credited with bringing it to Huntsville. He designed additions to many existing homes, but the most recognized legacy of George Steele is the large bank building located on Huntsville's Courthouse Square.

Although it was known as the Marble Palace at the time it was built, the State Bank at Huntsville, built in 1835, was made of limestone. The six Ionic columns were carried by barge down the Tennessee River after they were carved in Baltimore. The Greek revival masterpiece, with its gleaming white walls, was constructed high on the bluff above the Big Spring, the crowning jewel of Huntsville. The detailed carving and unusual features of the building were attributed to Steele's slaves, who were true artisans.

The bank had been built with living quarters for the cashier and his family. In addition, detention cells were built to house slaves held against their masters' debts. Debtors who did not own slaves were shackled there as well.

When war came to Huntsville in 1862, cashier Theophilus Lacy lived in the bank building with his family. His young son stood on the steps of the bank waving a Confederate flag as the Union troops moved in to occupy the city. A servant hastily snatched the child inside before his Southern patriotism caused a scene. According to legend, Lacy hid the bank notes inside the brick chimney and was threatened with execution by hanging if he didn't give them up. He never wavered, and fortunately he lived to resume his job after the war.

The Northern Bank of Alabama occupied the building by this time, and shortly after the Civil War, it became the National Bank of Huntsville. Theophilus Lacy kept his job with the new firm, and bank records dated January 22, 1867, stated that Mr. Lacy could bring his son Theo into the bank to help him—at no extra cost to the bank.

The bank building has served as a backdrop for many photographs over the years; some of the most well known are of soldiers standing at attention in front of it. It has also served as a backdrop for one of the most famous legends in Huntsville's history. Many people know the story of bandit Jesse James, who once robbed the bank. He leapt onto his horse, which was waiting outside the back entrance, and then made a dramatic leap over the bluff down into the Big Spring below. Some argue whether the horse suffered a broken leg in the escape. According to the story, the horse swam into a cave underneath the city and carried Jesse, with the bank's gold, to another entrance outside of town where they made their safe escape.

Of course, it was all made up. Jesse, as far as anyone can tell, never even visited Huntsville. His brother, Frank, on the other hand, was a guest of the city for a time while he stood trial for robbing the postal paymaster near Florence. But that is another story best left for another time.

George Steele and the Marble Palace

Over the decades, the bank has changed names several times. Several renovations have transformed the inside into a modern banking institution while retaining the charm of a previous century. Most recently, it was the property of Regions Bank. Although the building will remain standing, its future, at this time, remains unclear.

George Steele bought 320 acres and built Oak Place, his country home, in 1840. In March 1845, he sent out four thousand invitations to a party in honor of President James Polk. He commissioned a cake to be baked in Nashville with a figure of the president on it. He even sent his own wagon to Nashville to ensure the four-foot-tall cake's safe delivery. For each male guest, he had a special cane made from Monte Sano hickory. Special guests received a cane with a silver head on it.

Oak Place was occupied during the Civil War by Union troops. General Joe Wheeler used the home as his headquarters immediately following the Spanish-American War, while thousands of war veterans camped in Huntsville to recover from the effects of malaria and yellow fever they had suffered while serving in the Cuban jungles. Today, the home is well within the city limits of Huntsville, and the Maysville mansion has served as the home of East Huntsville Baptist Church since 1960.

After a long illness, George Steele died in 1855. He left debts and had long complained that two of his children "spent like there was no tomorrow." It was at that time that his will revealed a surprise that confirmed what may not have been much of a secret.

George Steele's will is recorded in Book 1 in the Madison County Records Room. Clause seven on page seventy-one contains the following entry:

I wish to set free a family of Negroes now slaves of mine; viz: Bet or Elizabeth, a mulatto woman aged about twenty-three years, also a mulatto boy named Ellis about nine years old, also a mulatto boy named John Brahan aged between seven and eight years, also a very bright mulatto boy named Charley, aged between two and three years, also a bright mulatto girl named Emma aged between one and two years. The four last are children of the said woman Bet or Elizabeth. I wish these servants removed to a free state, to either of the states of Ohio, Illinois or Michigan, and I wish them settled on a small farm in some economical orderly rural district in such free state; and the little farm or home to be stocked as may be necessary to be proportioned to the sum of money hereinafter specified. To this end I give and bequeath to the said mulatto woman, Bet or Elizabeth and her children...the sum of fifteen hundred dollars...being invested in the hands of my executor for the special benefit of the said woman and children so as to promote their comfort and support…I further direct that the expense of removing said woman and children…be borne by my estate and the sum of one hundred and twenty dollars additional to be appropriated out of my estate for a year's provisions for said family after they arrive in the free state. It is my wish that the provisions herein made for the removal of said woman and children may be carried into effect as soon as the circumstances of my estate will justify. And until the said woman and children are removed, it is my wish that they remain at the Fagan place where they now are, and to be well treated.

Although it was not stated in Steele's will, it is generally assumed that some or all of the children of Bet were also the children of George Steele. Within the last few years, some of his descendants came to Huntsville to research their ancestor. It was quite a surprise for them to discover that, although they had always assumed themselves to be white, they also descended from slaves.

Having children with a slave was nothing new in the antebellum South. Today, we can only speculate on the social aspects of that time, for very little information has been recorded regarding the thoughts of the plantation owner's wife or the slaves involved.

Within ten years of George Steele's death, everything changed for the family left in Huntsville. Financially, the family was ruined at the end of the War Between the States. Oak Place was auctioned in 1881 to pay debts and taxes. With the abolition of slavery, the plasterers, brick makers, carpenters and artisans were free to find their own work. History has not recorded what became of Steele's artisans; perhaps they created three-dimensional masterpieces in their own right. The most interesting unanswered question will probably remain unanswered: what became of twenty-three-year-old Elizabeth, the woman who was obviously much loved by a man named George Steele?

The Ghosts of the Forks of Cypress

June 6, 1966, started as an unusually hot and muggy day. By late afternoon, dark clouds had gathered in the sky and rain began to fall. An ominous stillness in the air alerted animals, and they began to grow restless. By nightfall, the angry roiling clouds opened, and sheets of rain pummeled the earth. White-hot bolts of lightning slashed through the dark sky. Across the Midwest and South, tornadoes touched down, leaving a wide swath of death and destruction. In Lauderdale County, Alabama, lightning struck the earth with ever-increasing frequency; each flash eerily illuminated a dark and empty mansion standing on a hill overlooking what was once an enormous plantation. It seemed as if Mother Nature was on a mission. Another flash of lightning streaked across the sky toward the earth, ending with an explosion of sparks. Within minutes, fire raged through the beautiful mansion. Flames licked the enormous columns, burning far more than wood, glass and plaster. The Forks of Cypress and over 140 years of history were gone—and, perhaps, the restless ghosts.

In the days before and after June 6, 1966, fifty-nine tornadoes touched down, leaving eighteen dead in the devastation. About four miles outside of Florence, Alabama, wisps of smoke rose from the smoldering ashes of an antebellum mansion. Twenty-three columns, two stories high, were all that remained, scorched but standing like silent, ever-vigilant sentries.

The man who built the mansion more than a century before, James Jackson, was born on October 25, 1782, in Creeve, County Monaghan, Ireland. James's mother died when he was only two years old, leaving eight

Forks of Cypress.

The Jackson family cemetery at the Forks of Cypress. *HABS-HAER photograph.*

young children, all under the age of thirteen, without a mother's love and gentle guiding hand. Jackson's widowed grandmother stepped in to help her son raise the young children. She lived an additional nine years, and shortly after her death, James left the stone two-story, ivy-covered house to live with his uncle in Dublin. He studied civil engineering, but his education ended abruptly with the Rebellion of 1799. Seventeen-year-old James escaped Ireland, along with his uncles Henry and John, to seek refuge first in Germany and then in the United States. After some time in Baltimore, James Jackson moved again. Records indicate that he was living in Nashville by 1804.

To say that James Jackson was ambitious and hardworking is an understatement. He had a mercantile business in Nashville and spent much time with another ambitious fellow with the same last name—Andrew Jackson. In 1810, James married a twenty-year-old widow with a young daughter. His attention soon turned to the fertile land in the Alabama Territory now opened up for sale. In 1817, General John Coffee, Supreme Justice John McKinley and James Jackson organized the Cypress Land Company and began a collaboration to lay out the town of Florence, Alabama. No doubt, his background in civil engineering served him well.

Jackson's own home was a masterpiece. While living temporarily in a log house, Jackson started his home in 1819 on a hill where, according to legend, a wigwam had once stood. The man who had lived in it was the Cherokee chief Doublehead.

The mansion, named the Forks of Cypress for the nearby Big and Little Cypress Creeks, took three years to complete. Twenty-four massive columns surrounded the home. They were constructed of pie-shaped bricks and mortared with a concoction of sand, molasses, charcoal and horsehair. The columns, wider at the bottom than at the top to give the optical illusion that they were much taller, were then covered with plaster. The finished home was stunning.

James Jackson had come a long way from his humble beginnings in Ireland. By the time Alabama was admitted into the Union as the twenty-second state, he was a wealthy man. James turned his attention to politics and a wealthy man's indulgence: horse racing. No doubt his interest in horses was influenced during his youth in Ireland. His uncle Hugh Jackson owned an award-winning mare named Jane, and family lore claims that upon the mare's death, she was buried just outside Hugh Jackson's door.

James Jackson was serious about his horses and the sport of racing. He had a racetrack built on his three-thousand-acre cotton plantation. Three horses were imported from England: Glencoe (once owned by King George IV), Leviathan and Pocahontas. Some of the finest racehorses were bred from them, and an amazing fourteen descendants of Glencoe went on to win the Kentucky Derby. Peytona, sired by Glencoe, had a stride of twenty-seven feet, and she remained undefeated for some time. In a wager to settle which region of the country raised superior racehorses, Peytona was chosen to race against her northern equivalent, a mare named Fashion. Peytona was led by a stableboy to Long Island, New York, from Florence to represent the South. This famous race, which occurred on May 15, 1845, was so important that the artists Nathaniel Currier and James Merritt Ives were present to record the event in color. Carrier pigeons waited to carry the results to New York newspapers. It was estimated that a crowd of 100,000 people would come to see the historic race. Peytona did not disappoint the people of the South. She won the race, and the newspapers had the results within nine minutes of the finish.

Peytona's win did not come without sacrifice. Immediately after the race, her front legs were declared to be feverish, and she did not compete in the Jockey Club Purse days later. When she next competed against Fashion, she was defeated, and soon it became clear that Peytona's racing days were behind her.

Although James Jackson watched the early progress of Peytona after her birth, he did not live long enough to appreciate Peytona's famous victory. He died in August 1840 at the age of fifty-eight. His newspaper obituary gave a detailed account of Jackson's unexpected death:

> *He departed this life suddenly on Monday last, between the hours of twelve and one o'clock in the 58th year of his age. Mr. J. had experienced, a week or two before his death, a violent and dangerous attack of fever, but had recovered from it sufficiently to take moderate exercise, and on that fatal morning rode out upon his plantation as was his custom when in health. It is probably however, that in this occasion he presumed too far upon his restoration and his naturally robust and stirring habits—he returned to the house with a chilly, full sensation, and before one o'clock was a corpse.*

Over two decades later, much of North Alabama was occupied by Federal forces in the Civil War. Colonel James Jackson Jr., who was forty at the beginning of the war, had inherited his father's fearlessness and love of beauty. Although he was educated at Princeton and a member of a prominent family, he enlisted in the Confederate army as a private in the Fourth Alabama

Infantry. Jackson was shot in the chest in the first Battle of Manassas and sent home. After his recovery, he organized the Twenty-seventh Alabama Infantry and was commissioned a lieutenant colonel. He, along with most of his company, was captured at Fort Donelson in February 1862. After seven months in the Johnson's Island prison camp, he was exchanged. Jackson took over as colonel of his regiment upon the death of Colonel A.A. Hughes and went on to Vicksburg, where he and his men remained until July 1863. Interestingly, while in Vicksburg, he ordered his men to fix their bayonets and charge a Georgia regiment as it needlessly trampled the flowers of a private home. The Georgians backed off immediately and were no doubt surprised at Jackson's need to preserve a little beauty in the midst of chaos.

By 1864, about 150 members of the Ninth Ohio, riding white horses, occupied part of Lauderdale County, harassing and living off the civilians. Colonel Jackson had been informed that they were living in and around the Forks of Cypress, where his widowed mother also lived. Jackson quickly gathered together his most fearsome and trusted men to cross over enemy lines and run them out. On the night of April 11, he and his men ferried across Tuscumbia Landing on the Tennessee River and took a slave guide, who informed them that it was actually the home of Jack Peters that was occupied. They crept quietly on, avoiding the roads, until they were within 150 yards of the campfires of members of the White Horse Company. At the signal, they charged, firing their weapons and yelling the name of the dreaded Nathan Bedford Forrest, sure to strike fear into the hearts and minds of the enemy. Forty-two prisoners were taken along with forty-four white horses. Jackson ordered that the mules and cattle taken from local civilians be turned loose in the fields in the hope that they would return to their owners. James Jackson Jr. survived the war and died in 1879 at age fifty-seven.

The mansion survived the Civil War as well and continued on as one of the showpieces of architecture in Lauderdale County. Along with the survival of the mansion came an increasing number of stories of ghosts haunting the estate. In the early 1960s, the late Faye Axford, a well-known writer and historian from nearby Athens, visited the mansion on several occasions. Each time, there were unexplained occurrences.

During her first visit, Faye settled in for the night in one of the guest bedrooms. Sometime shortly after she drifted off to sleep, the door to her bedroom slammed shut. She quickly opened her eyes and cautiously looked about the darkened room. After a few minutes, assured that she was indeed alone, she was overtaken by sleep once again. A woman's scream startled her into consciousness, and this time, her nerves were rattled. Within a short time, she was once again shaken by the loud blast of a gunshot in the darkness. She did not sleep for the rest of the night.

The next morning, Faye wandered downstairs, bleary-eyed and exhausted. Her host was surprised when she told him of her sleepless night, but when she told him what had happened, he had an explanation. The slamming of the door was caused when the air conditioner came on. The woman's scream was not a woman at all but a neighbor's peacock wandering past the home, making much the same sound as a woman. The gunshot was explained with an apology. The host had fired his gun in order to scare off local students of Florence State who frequently drove out for late-night beer sessions.

While the events of her first night were easily explained away, none of Faye's other experiences could be dismissed in the same manner. On another visit, Faye had settled in to her guest room, and while rummaging through her purse, she accidentally dropped her wallet behind the dresser, where it slipped down to the floor. She started to retrieve it but was called down to supper with the others guests. She made a mental note to remember to find it when she returned. But after a pleasant meal, she returned to her room only to discover the wallet lying on top of the dresser. Faye asked her host who had gone to the trouble to get it for her so she could properly thank him. Her host had no idea what she was talking about, and the subject had not been discussed at supper that night. Perhaps it was the ghost of a tall stately woman that was known to walk the halls and grounds near the home. The ghost was said to wear old-fashioned clothing and seemed to be in search of something—or someone.

It could have been the ghost of Parson Dick, the slave who served as the butler inside the mansion. He was married, but his wife lived on a nearby plantation, which he frequently visited. During the Union occupation, Parson Dick rode a horse one day to pay a visit to his wife. He never arrived at his destination and was never seen or heard from again. Is he lost, looking for his way, or is he trying to communicate the mystery of his fate? Or could the ghost be that of a mulatto slave named Queen, thought to be the daughter of James Jackson Jr., who left the Forks of Cypress at the end of the Civil War, traveled to Decatur and went to Tennessee? Although Queen was treated differently—perhaps a little better than most of the Jackson family slaves—her father did not acknowledge her as his daughter. The beautiful former slave was the grandmother of writer Alex Haley, whose family stories were incorporated into his novels. It would make sense that, given the history of the home and the number of people who once lived there, more than a few ghosts remained.

The Ghosts of the Forks of Cypress

Columns are all that remain of the Forks of Cypress. *Photo courtesy Patrick Hood of Patrick Hood Photography.*

On the occasion of Faye's next visit, she was shown to a different guest room. She put down her suitcase and laughingly made a comment out loud, something to the effect of, "I suppose I will not be staying with the ghost in the other room tonight." No sooner had the words come out of her mouth than a cut-glass candy dish flew across a table and clattered loudly onto the floor. She was shaken by the response of whatever, or whomever, she had encountered—but not enough to stay away. She was invited again to visit the Forks of Cypress and gladly accepted. She did not make that trip, however, because she planned to arrive on June 7, 1966—the day after the home burned to the ground.

About the Author

Jacquelyn Procter Reeves is a native of Las Vegas, New Mexico, and a graduate of New Mexico Highlands University. She is the editor of North Alabama's *Valley Leaves* and associate editor of *Old Tennessee Valley Magazine* in Decatur. Jacque is the curator of the historic Donnell House in Athens and owner of Avalon Tours in Huntsville.

She conducts ghost walks, cemetery tours and historic tours and has served on Huntsville's Maple Hill Cemetery Stroll committee for some fourteen years. She teaches history to students all over the United States via distance learning through Early Works Museum in Huntsville. In her spare time, she has written scores of short stories and nine books and has served as contributing writer to many others. Jacque lives in Huntsville.

Visit us at
www.historypress.net